A Stylish Guide to
CLASSIC SEWING

Sarah Gunn and Julie Starr

Explore 30 Timeless
Garments with History,
Styling & Tips for
Ready-to-Wear Results

C&T PUBLISHING

Text copyright © 2019 by Sarah Gunn and Julie Starr

Photography and artwork copyright © 2019 by C&T Publishing, Inc.

PUBLISHER: Amy Marson

CREATIVE DIRECTOR: Gailen Runge

ACQUISITIONS EDITOR: Roxane Cerda

MANAGING EDITOR: Liz Aneloski

EDITOR: Beth Baumgartel

TECHNICAL EDITOR: Linda Johnson

COVER/BOOK DESIGNER: April Mostek

PRODUCTION COORDINATOR: Tim Manibusan

PRODUCTION EDITOR: Alice Mace Nakanishi

COVER/FASHION ILLUSTRATOR: Beth Briggs

GRADED-PATTERN ILLUSTRATOR: Jennifer DeShazer
of Jennuine Designs

INSTRUCTIONAL ILLUSTRATOR: Linda Johnson

STYLE PHOTOGRAPHERS: Andrea Birkan,
Cennetta Burwell, Karon Cooke-Euter,
Alexandra Florea, Jacqueline Foley, William Gunn,
Emily Hallman, Thomas B. Helm, Allie Jackson,
Jenna Ledawn, Duong Nguyen Lengerer,
Martin Mogaard, Anita Morris, Philip Nittala /
Manju Nittala, Dorcas Ross, Chris Smith,
Lori VanMaanen, and Vatsla Watkins

PHOTO ASSISTANT: Rachel Holmes

Published by C&T Publishing, Inc., P.O. Box 1456, Lafayette, CA 94549

Library of Congress Cataloging-in-Publication Data

Names: Gunn, Sarah, 1956- author. | Starr, Julie, 1957- author.

Title: A stylish guide to classic sewing : explore 30 timeless garments with history, styling & tips
for ready-to-wear results / Sarah Gunn and Julie Starr.

Description: Lafayette, CA : C&T Publishing, Inc., [2019] | Includes bibliographical references.

Identifiers: LCCN 2019020879 | ISBN 9781617458729 (softcover)

Subjects: LCSH: Tailoring. | Sewing.

Classification: LCC TT580 .G86 2019 | DDC 646.4--dc23

LC record available at https://lccn.loc.gov/2019020879

Printed in China

10 9 8 7 6 5 4 3 2 1

Dedication

We dedicate this book to …

These unforgettable style icons who recognized the simple elegance of classic garments. Thank you for teaching us how to dress!

PRINCESS DIANA · AUDREY HEPBURN · KATHARINE HEPBURN · GRACE KELLY · JACQUELINE KENNEDY
MARY TYLER MOORE · MARLO THOMAS

These talented fashion designers, for creating beautiful, timeless classics.

OLEG CASSINI · COCO CHANEL · CHRISTIAN DIOR · DIANE VON FURSTENBERG · HUBERT DE GIVENCHY
CAROLINA HERRERA · EDITH HEAD · CALVIN KLEIN · RALPH LAUREN · YVES SAINT LAURENT · CLAIRE MCCARDELL
OSCAR DE LA RENTA · LILLY PULITZER · KATE SPADE · KARL LAGERFELD · TRACY REESE

To all present-day designers who have reimagined the classics with a contemporary twist.

Acknowledgments

A special thank-you to …

- Beth Briggs, whose delightful fashion illustrations capture the whimsical spirit of classical clothing.

- The talented designers featured in the photo gallery, for sharing their creative interpretations of the classics.

- The online sewing community that inspires us every day by sharing the creativity and originality of a hand-curated wardrobe.

- Beth Baumgartel, the editor of our dreams! Your help has been invaluable in every way.

- Katie Burris, our photo stylist with a keen eye for details.

- Chris Smith, our friend and photographer extraordinaire.

- Pixel Studios in Charleston, South Carolina, for providing us with a great venue for our fashion shoot.

- Jennifer DeShazer for her invaluable technical assistance with the Modern Classic Pencil Skirt pattern.

- Billy Gunn, for his continuing support and encouragement.

- The dedicated staff at C&T Publishing for turning our dreams into reality.

- Mood Fabrics, for its continuous generosity in providing fabrics to the *Goodbye Valentino* blog; Lynn Browne from Coats & Clark, Inc., for thread galore and the many opportunities to share Sarah's ideas and projects; and PFAFF, for making our sewing experience most enjoyable!

Contents

THE CLASSIC GARMENT GALLERY 76

Foreword

In the 1950s, fashion legend Claire McCardell urged young design students to cultivate an eye for style, then use it to create a modern, practical, yet chic wardrobe, with a little help from a sewing machine. "Learn to see—learn to sew," she told them.

Back then, women carefully curated their wardrobes. They chose clothing and accessories that worked together as coordinating outfits to be worn and updated from year to year. Some clothes were bought, some were sewn, and some were thriftily repurposed from other garments. Their clothes were well-made and well-maintained, and lasted for years.

When I was a teen, my mom taught me to look through my closet in the fall and decide on a few new garments to round out my wardrobe for school and activities. What we couldn't find in our northern Michigan town—particularly the young, hip, designer fashions of the 70s—she showed me how to sew. Planning, creating, and maintaining my wardrobe became a great source of pleasure for me, and a way to express creativity and style!

Unfortunately, the recent era of fast fashion has brought ill-fitting, poorly-made clothing to stores, which people buy on a whim and toss out just as easily. It's bad for the environment and a disaster for style. Somewhere along the way, we lost the ability to build a wardrobe with quality pieces that go together.

Enter Sarah Gunn, creator of the popular "Ready-to-Wear Fast" through her blog, *Goodbye Valentino*, and Julie Starr, an inspirational sewist who is a cheerleader for the craft via Pattern Review and other online communities. Through their books, Julie and Sarah are encouraging people around the world to sew flattering, beautiful fashions that are "built to last."

The styles in this book are classics because they've stood the test of time and are reborn with every generation. The pencil skirt, for example, was worn by the modern gals in 1930's movies, then the silhouette got tighter as part of the "sweater girl" uniform in the 50s. It flattered Princess Di in the 80s and is still making a style statement—more than 30 years later—on her daughters-in-law Kate Middleton and Meghan Markle.

When you make yourself a "modern classic pencil skirt," with Julie and Sarah's expert advice on fabric, fitting, and sewing, you're on your way to creating a unique, made-for-you wardrobe that takes you from the local Starbucks to Paris! Whether you learned to sew when you were a child, as I did, or as part of the more recent #makersmovement, a chic wardrobe is doable on any budget, with a bit of knowledge, creativity, and a sewing machine.

And did I mention it was fun? Nowadays, as we plan and create our projects, we can go online to share our successes (and frustrations) with our new "sewing friends" who live anywhere from Charleston to Sydney. When possible, we meet up in person to spread our love of the craft. This modern-day virtual "sewing circle" has grown into a worldwide community of makers, bonding across cultures and time zones.

So, kudos to Sarah and Julie for updating Claire McCardell's advice about "seeing and sewing," and for encouraging us to have some fun stitching up these classic, fashionable looks. May this book inspire you to plan and sew a timeless, chic, quality wardrobe—a long-lost luxury that every woman deserves!

JULIE EILBER

Courtesy of Julie Eilber

Julie Eilber is a writer and sewing enthusiast known for re-creating vintage designer fashions by Chanel, Charles James, Schiaparelli, and Claire McCardell, which she shares on her irreverent blog, *Jet Set Sewing*. A sewing expert for BERNINA USA, she's created tutorials and patterns for its website and has written profiles of couturiers Susan Khalje and Kenneth D. King. As a fashion historian, she's presented workshops at the Museum of Modern Art and has been published in *The Journal of Dress History*.

Introduction

Sew your own clothes, save thousands of dollars,
and look like a million bucks!

Dear Readers,

Congratulations! You are either sewing your own clothes or contemplating the idea. Either choice is a winner because you believe—or hope—an alternative to shopping for ready-to-wear clothing exists.

Whether you are seeking economical relief, a fit that flatters your shape, styles that reflect your taste, or a general creative outlet, sewing your clothes provides all of the above. Our re-entry into the fashion sewing scene began with the goal to save money, but soon we learned to fit ourselves and people took notice of our flattering clothes.

"Did you lose weight?" *or* "Whose design are you wearing?" *and* "That is the most beautiful color."

Once people learned we sewed, the comments changed to, "You are so talented!" *or* "My grandmother sewed!" *and even* "I wish I could sew."

If you can read a recipe, you can read pattern instructions. If you can drive a car, you can operate a sewing machine, and if you can spend hours upon hours shopping and returning clothes, you have time to sew.

Through the years we have sewn hundreds of garments from commercial patterns and countless tunics (page 40) from our book, *The Tunic Bible* (page 176). We conclude the key to sewing a successful wardrobe is constructing pieces you will wear over and over again, and we begin with the classics.

We wrote *A Stylish Guide to Classic Sewing* to trigger sewing mojo and awaken your personal style by presenting 30 timeless garments which have endured the test of time and carried dozens of trends through the decades. Whether you are an aspiring or dedicated home sewer, our book will serve as your guide to sewing a functional and fashionable wardrobe.

Every prominent designer understands the concept of classic garments before stepping on to the runway. When we know how to adapt garments to suit our style, age, shape, and size, we are a step ahead of seasonal trends. Sewists get the best of both worlds by applying the designer's essence to clothes that work for their lifestyle.

Classic garments are designed to flatter everyone when properly fitted. Take the button-up shirt for example. With a proper fit or a few adjustments, this style works on every shape and size. But when a garment doesn't fit, we believe the style is not meant for us.

Patterns may come and go, but style is eternal!

The Classic Garment Gallery (page 76), found in the center section of the book, is filled with photographs of the 30 classics, modeled and sewn by popular online sewists. While we identify the name of each garment, a particular sewing pattern is not crucial to your success, since commercial pattern companies offer continuous selections of the classics.

Variety is the spice of life!

To highlight the significant role these classic garments play in a functional and fashionable ward-robe, we dedicate a chapter to each of the 30 classics. Beth Briggs's illustrated variations capture the beauty of achieving major results from small imaginative changes and inspire us to think beyond the pattern.

Sew like a pro!

As a bonus, we include our Modern Classic Pencil Skirt pattern (pullout page P1), a full-size pattern sizes 2–22, along with leading tips on achieving sought-after ready-to-wear results.

With constantly changing trends, it's easy to be confused about our clothing choices, but look closely—the trendy shirt with the sleeve of the moment began with a classic button-up design, and the color-block dress is an A-line silhouette.

Knowing which garments to sew is the first step in creating your customized wardrobe. As we reflect on classic garments, we are drawn to archetypal designs—the blueprints of fashion that continue to evolve and inspire today's fashion trends. Our list of 30 classics follows:

1. A-Line Skirt

2. Gored Skirt

3. Pencil Skirt

4. Full Skirt

5. Button-Up Shirt

6. T-Shirt

7. Turtleneck

8. Bateau Neckline Top and Dress

9. Tunic

10. Cardigan Sweater

11. Twin Sweater Set

12. Shift Dress

13. Sheath Dress

14. A-Line Dress

15. Trapeze Dress

16. Fit and Flare Dress

17. Wrap Dress

18. Shirtdress

19. Halter Dress or Top

20. Jeans

21. Fitted and Straight Tailored Trousers

22. Wide-Leg and Flared Tailored Trousers

23. Palazzo Pants

24. Capri Pants

25. Jeans-Style Jacket

26. Blazer

27. Trench Coat

28. French Jacket

29. Menswear Pajamas

30. Wraps

Knowing what to do with a pattern is the first step in developing your personal style. After browsing through our list of 30 classics, take a look in your closet. What works? Did you buy any clothes out of desperation? Do your clothes fit? Do you need more variety, or is your style all over the place? Do you wish you could find your favorite skirt silhouette in red?

When you combine the principals of classic design and proper fitting with the fabrics and details that reflect your personality, your comfort level will skyrocket, your wardrobe will change, and you will walk through life with originality and runway confidence!

Skirts

A-Line and Gored Skirts

Whether your style is a preppy tartan plaid or a sequin mini, you'll want an A-line in your future! The classic A-line silhouette flatters several body shapes by creating the illusion of a small waist, camouflaging large thighs and hips, and giving a feminine vibe to boyish figures. Sew it as a mini, midi, or maxi!

"I start each collection thinking how I can refresh the classics." JEAN PAUL GAULTIER

History

While baby boomers learned to sew a modest A-line skirt in home economics classes, millennials flaunt this simple frock from maxi to bootie length. The A-line skirt is a must-sew for beginners or any sewist seeking to rekindle their sewing mojo. Starting with this simple garment introduces you to the benefits of the customized fit you've been seeking!

Easy to fit and easy to wear, the A-line silhouette was originally introduced as a dress by Christian Dior in his 1955 "A" collection. The A-line silhouette was a significant departure from Dior's previous "New Look" collections featuring nipped in waists and dramatically fitted details. As fashion styles evolved, the A-line skirt became a popular garment on its own, often paired with closely fitted tops with narrow shoulders and fitted sleeves. We credit the flight attendants of the late 1950s and early 1960s for popularizing the style in their chic designer uniform ensembles. Leading fashion designers including Pierre Cardin, Emilio Pucci, and Coco Chanel created these ensembles specifically for the airlines featuring lots of trendy A-lines. Just imagine, a Chanel flight attendant uniform!

Characteristics

A-line, just like the letter, describes the shape of a skirt or dress, wider around the hips than at the waist. It is fitted from the natural waist to the upper hip with darts and gradually widens to the hem. The skirt is generally closed with a side or back zipper. A waistband is optional, and nicely secures a tucked-in top. Waistbands also provide added detail; try sewing a horizontally striped skirt with a vertically striped waistband to create visual interest.

Sewing Tips

- When sewing an A-line skirt, fit the pattern around the waist with just enough wearing ease to walk, sit, and bend comfortably. Too much ease in a waistband suggests the appearance of a larger waistline.

- If you are sewing with woven fabric, lining your A-line helps prevent wearing wrinkles and doesn't require a lot of extra sewing time.

- A-line patterns with a side zipper feature two pieces (front and back), while patterns with a back zipper feature three pieces (front and two backs) and provide greater fitting control. We recommend using a two-piece pattern for light-weight fabrics or complex fabric designs like plaids. Heavier fabrics sew nicely in both two- and three-piece patterns.

- A-line patterns designed for knits often feature an elastic waistband and don't require a zipper closure. When using this type of pattern, look for one that features the flat elastic insertion method to avoid waistline gathers.

Fabric Suggestions

The classic A-line adapts to the fabric spectrum; almost all fabrics work to make this simple garment a wardrobe mainstay. Some of our favorite choices are wool crepe, cotton broadcloth, denim, heavier silks, lace, suede, and even home-dec fabric! Border prints, large florals, stripes, and geometrics bring this style to life!

The Frump Factor

Choose the right length for your skirt. If a mini skirt is not age appropriate, find a length around the knee for everyday styling. Unless you're deliberately choosing a midi length, too long can look frumpy!

The Gored Skirt

The gored skirt is a variation of the classic A-line. A great option for skirt makers, the gored skirt is sewn from several triangular-shaped pieces of fabric, known as gores (panels). The gores are smaller at the top (near the waist) and wider toward the bottom (hem) creating an A-line shape when the gores are stitched together.

Its early silhouette was reminiscent of the Victorian bustled era until Coco Chanel reinvented the silhouette by working a little magic on its flattering shape and simple seaming. By reducing the scale of the triangle and alternating metallic boucle panels with solid wool panels, Chanel created wearable works of art from its ho-hum past.

How to Style

- Pairing an A-line skirt with a traditional blazer is an easy way to dress professionally. Check the proportions of the jacket and skirt together so your silhouette is flattering and pleasing to you. Look for a continuous line from the jacket to the skirt.

- The A-line skirt pairs beautifully with fitted shirts, turtlenecks, or simple tops worn with statement jewelry.

- A-line skirts work with every type of shoe from flip-flops to boots. Your choice of shoes depends on fabric selection and accessories.

- Pair a tropical print skirt with a T-shirt and flip flops for casual daywear and a sleeveless silk top and gold sandals for evening.

- A-lines sewn from heavily textured fabrics and boots go hand-in-hand.

- Try layering a midi-length overlay over a shorter and narrower A-line skirt.

Who Wore It

It's the skirt that keeps on giving! You'll find the A-line a staple wardrobe item on your favorite 60's television shows, as well as on today's pop stars.

MARLO THOMAS · CHERYL TIEGS · TWIGGY · JEAN SHRIMPTON · PEGGY LIPTON · THE SUPREMES
CYBILL SHEPHERD · SUZANNE PLESHETTE in *The Birds* · 1960 AIRLINE "STEWARDESS" · TAYLOR SWIFT
JESSICA ALBA · ANNE HATHAWAY

Pencil Skirt

It's true, a pencil skirt is not just for pencil-thin women! While the skirt has gone through multiple evolutions, its figure-hugging shape has remained the same. This no-frill feminine garment flatters many figure types and conveys confidence wherever it goes. Its perpetual appeal keeps it at the top of the classics list.

"A good speech should be like a woman's skirt: long enough to cover the subject and short enough to create interest." WINSTON CHURCHILL

History

It's hard to believe Orville and Wilbur Wright are credited with inventing the predecessor to the pencil skirt—known as *the hobble skirt*. When the first female passenger accompanied the Wright brothers on a flight in 1908, they quickly discovered her long, full skirt was in danger of getting caught in the propellers, so they tied a rope around her ankles that forced her to hobble when she walked. The flight received immense media attention and the skirt became a short-lived fashion trend.

Christian Dior introduced the first pencil skirt in the 1940s as part of a suit. Due to wartime rations and fabric shortages, hemlines rose to calf length and slimmer silhouettes prevailed, but it was his 1954 "H" collection that garnered international fame for the pencil skirt. Leading starlets rocked the look, and women embraced the feminine and shapely new fashion. What debuted as the bottom half of a suit was soon a stand-alone garment that eventually found its place as an office mainstay.

Characteristics

The classic pencil skirt is slim-fitting with a knee-length hemline and a back vent or slit. Although the skirt appears straight like a pencil, a well-cut pencil skirt features a subtle bell shape to accentuate a woman's curves. The skirt is sewn with or without a waistband, but the top of the skirt rests on the waist. The original hemline of the first pencil skirts from the 1940s hit just below the knee, but over the years the hemline has risen and fallen with changing trends.

Sewing Tips

We designed our Modern Classic Pencil Skirt pattern (pullout page P1) with our favorite characteristics in mind. The subtle bell shape, dartless front, and three-piece shaped waistband provide the feminine flair a pencil skirt deserves!

- When sewing with woven fabrics, pencil skirts are best underlined or lined to minimize wrinkles and preserve the shape.

- Waistbands are a matter of preference. If you sew a pencil skirt without a waistband, stabilize the waist with Petersham ribbon (see Resources: Trims, Tools, and Notions, page 174).

- Always select a pattern with a back split or vent for knee length and longer skirts so you can walk with ease.

- Your pencil skirt should be fitted—not tight, but snug. In the sewing industry, a fitted skirt allows 2″–3″ (5–7.5 cm) of ease through the hips.

- Make sure your zipper is long enough to open the skirt comfortably so it doesn't strain as you put it on and take it off.

Fabric Suggestions

Midweight fabrics such as bouclé, wool crepe, gabardine, tweeds, twill, and stable knits produce beautiful pencil skirts. Stretch fabrics, with the addition of Lycra, spandex, or elastane, are used to make closer fitting skirts without the need of a back vent. Be sure to choose a compatible lining such as mesh or tricot that stretches with the stretch fabric. And, if you are feeling adventurous, go bold with leather, lace, or sequined fabrics—no one will believe you made it.

How to Style

- If you like heels, the pencil skirt is your garment! Think pumps, kitten heels, booties, sandals, and stilettos!

- To balance the look of a leather pencil skirt, try a top with a high neckline and long sleeves.

- Create an ethereal mood by pairing a delicate fabric top with a light floral pencil skirt.

- Lace pencil skirts and silk tops are made for each other!

- Chunky wool tweeds always work with sweater sets and a bold necklace.

- Need we say the perfect mate to a bouclé pencil skirt is a French jacket (page 153)?

- For professional needs, think beyond the solid navy suit and make the pencil skirt in a subtle plaid.

- Try sewing a piqué skirt with a scalloped edge fabric for your next resort vacation.

- You can never go wrong with a black pencil skirt. The endless styling options will take you wherever you need to go. To quote Neiman Marcus, "Women who wear black lead colorful lives."

Who Wore It

From the *Mad Men* series and Washington politicians to red carpet parties and evenings at the club, pencil skirts are major players in our society.

We can thank these ladies for making the pencil skirt a classic:

AVA GARDNER · MARILYN MONROE · AUDREY HEPBURN · PRINCESS GRACE · LONI ANDERSON

Full Skirt

Oozing in romance from the nostalgic golden era of old Hollywood, the classic full skirt continues to convey time-less femininity and grace. Practical and pretty, its fullness downplays larger hips and slims the waistline appear-ance. The wider the skirt the more magical the effect! Introduce this class act into your wardrobe and rekindle the mystique of feminine charm!

"Elegance is about restraint." BRANDON MAXWELL

History

During the Antebellum and Victorian eras, long, full skirts with lavish ornamentation defined luxury and status, mainly because fabric and trims were prized and considered precious and expensive. Not only were skirts worn for modesty, their prestige increased incrementally accord-ing to the volume of fabric between the waistline and hem! The skirt circumference race was on—bustles, hoops, petticoats, and crinolines were employed to create a silhouette meant to impress! Of course, this was at the expense of women's comfort and safety. No doubt these poor ladies suffered from aching backs, not to mention a great weariness of standing!

Christian Dior's 1947 "New Look" set the tone for the next decade. With tightly cinched waists and billowing skirts, his full, circular, or pleated styles were supported by layered net petticoats to give lift (made of lighter synthetics like nylon) and were popular for daytime dressing, as well as eveningwear.

We still adore full skirts and pronounce them both practical and pretty, an ideal choice for time-less femininity and grace.

Characteristics

The classic full skirt is gathered or pleated into a waistband or facing and beautifully balances the figure by creating an hourglass effect. Bias-cut full skirts gently glide to glory without the need for pleats and gathers. Drop-waisted full skirts or styles constructed with a yoke from which soft pleats or gathers flow diminish the fullness directly at the waistline.

Sewing Tips

- Mark pleats carefully using your method of choice and baste them in place with two parallel rows of stitching to avoid shifting fabric layers.

- Depending on your desired fullness, you can tame waistline bulk with weightier fabrics by stitching the pleats down for 3″–6″ (7.5–15cm) from the waistband. Stitched and released pleats are fabulously slimming.

- Special pleating boards make short work of sewing evenly spaced knife pleats with a fast and easy tuck, press, and sew method. These are readily available at sewing supply stores and websites (see Resources: Fabric Vendors, page 173). Use white vinegar and a press cloth to set in permanent pleats that won't wash away.

- Pockets are one of our favorite features and are almost always found in full skirts! If your pattern doesn't include them, they're easy to add in the side seams. Simply use a pocket pattern from your favorite sewing or commercial pattern. If you are making your skirt with medium- to heavier-weight fabrics, choose a lighter-weight fabric for the pockets to eliminate excess bulk. We love pockets that are deep enough to stash our phone and a lipstick!

- Horsehair braid is a useful notion to add extra body to hems without stiffness (see Resources: Trims, Tools, and Notions, page 174).

Fabric Suggestions

From broadcloth to brocade, the full skirt can be made from a multitude of fabrics, perhaps something already in your fabric stash! The flowing volume of the skirt pairs well with lightweight voile, shirting, linen, seersucker, and silk for a warm season skirt—no lining required! For a bit more structure, with all the same sashay, cotton sateen, lightweight denim, and stable knits are all great choices. Painterly, panel, or border prints are great choices for a skirt that's sure to be noticed. This is a style that can showcase bold, large-scale patterns!

For eveningwear, silk dupioni, lace, jacquard, velvet, satin, taffeta, and brocade are sumptuous choices with texture, shimmer, and shine.

If you decide to line your full skirt, we recommend china silk, crepe de chine, Bemberg rayon, and charmeuse—either polyester, or, for a true tactile treat, silk charmeuse.

How to Style

- Proportion and balance are the two most important details to keep in mind when sewing and wearing full skirted styles.

- For unfailing elegance, wear a full-bodied skirt Carolina Herrera–style with a sleekly darted white shirt.

- Keep the ladylike vibe going by adding a silky blouse and dainty pumps.

- Give your ensemble some edge by rocking a cropped leather moto jacket and a pair of ankle boots with your skirt.

- For a romantic boho feel, wear a swishy, flounced floral midi or maxi length full skirt using a simple and quick-to-make elastic casing waistband. Cowboy boots and a statement-belted flowing top are a great counterpoint to keep it all from looking too precious.

- Bold, wide horizontal stripes in high-contrast colors are a fresh and modern take on classic full skirt styles.

The Frump Factor

Avoid the frump factor by carefully considering shoe selection for the length of your skirt. Try a hem just at or below the knee with a high heel to lengthen your legs. If you're tall, a longer skirt with ballet flats will accentuate your legs without showing too much skin.

Who Wore It

Full, voluminous skirts are more popular than ever! These exuberant ladies have kept the look alive throughout the decades.

CAROLINA HERRERA • LUCILLE BALL
GRACE KELLY • NINA RICCI • ELIZABETH TAYLOR
OLIVIA NEWTON-JOHN in *Grease*
ANNETTE FUNICELLO • TAYLOR SWIFT
CYBILL SHEPHERD

Tops

Button-Up Shirt

What other tailored garment is at home in the boardroom or in the bedroom or everywhere in between? The universal white shirt is an absolute must-have, but don't stop there. The classic button-up shirt conveys any style you're seeking—chic, prim, proper, romantic, sophisticated, rugged, intellectual, professional!

"When I don't know what to wear I chose a white shirt—you can wear a white shirt with anything." CAROLINA HERRERA

History

This classic shirt has a history worthy of its own encyclopedia! Originally designed as underwear to protect men's dress coats from soiling, the modern shirt is traced to Edwardian times. Through the centuries a detailed etiquette of shirt attire evolved—how many buttons and when to button, collar dimensions, shirttail lengths, barrel cuffs or French cuffs or single cuffs, when to wear what color, and what fabric was suitable for particular times of the day.

Brooks Brothers introduced the button-down shirt at the turn of the twentieth century. The button-down collar was originally referred to as a *sports collar*, modeled after shirts worn by polo players. While attending a polo match in England, Mr. Brooks noticed the players had stitched small buttons onto their shirt collars to keep the collar from flapping in their faces. Brooks took the idea back to the United States, tweaked the collar and a classic was born.

As women began to enter the workforce, a new shirt trend emerged: the *button-up* shirt. The difference between the button-up and the button-down shirt lies strictly in the collar. The button-down shirt's collar buttons to the shirt front, while the button-up shirt's collar has no buttons and remains free.

One distinct detail differentiates a woman's shirt from a man's: Women's shirts feature buttons on the left and buttonholes on the right, while men's shirts feature buttons on the right and buttonholes on the left.

Fashion designers such as Ralph Lauren and Carolina Herrera have secured a permanent place on the runway for the classic shirt, and no wardrobe should be without one!

Characteristics

Traditional classic woven-fabric shirts feature the following elements: a one-piece back sewn to a yoke; one-piece sleeves with plackets at the wrist; cuffs; a turndown pointed collar; and front plackets that button closed. Once women began wearing menswear shirts, clothing designers feminized the silhouette, shaping them with darts or princess seams.

Sewing Tips

* We never wore button-down or button-up shirts before we started sewing, but now we sew and wear these classics all the time. Ready-to-wear shirts fit very few women perfectly, but the good news is shirt alterations are easily achievable. Sewing the shirt components is quite technical and requires precision throughout, so we have listed several books and tutorials to guide you through the process of both fitting and sewing the details with confidence. (See Resources: Related Articles, Videos, and Online Classes, page 174, and Sewing Instruction and Alteration Books, page 175.)

* For better sewing control, we recommend hand stitching the inside collar band and sleeve cuffs. You can finish with a topstitch if desired.

* When placing your buttons on the front placket, place the first button at the fullest part of the bust and space the remaining buttons up and down from there. This eliminates gaping along the placket and allows more styling opportunities.

Fabric Suggestions

Classic shirts are sewn from woven materials. Natural fibers such as cotton and linen, woven into fabrics such as poplin, broadcloth, Oxford cloth, denim, linen fabric, and flannel are excellent choices. Fabric blends of cotton, polyester, and rayon work well, although 100% polyester does not offer the breathability of natural fibers, but it is very durable. Today's stretch blend fabrics make excellent choices and sometimes minimize fit issues. Silks make beautiful button-up shirts, but should be tackled by sewists with advanced skill sets.

In addition to solid colors, designs such as plaid, gingham, stripes, and floral are great choices.

Design Variations

The classic shirt lends itself to several design variations.

Think about …

… omitting the collar and finishing with the collar stand only.

… sewing a high-low hem, or giving the body a slightly A-line shape with a handkerchief hem.

… making it sleeveless or substituting butterfly sleeves, open ruffle cuffs, or 1˝ (2.5 cm) tie cuffs.

… embellishing with monograms or embroidery on the collar, cuffs, or pockets.

… adding whimsy with contrasting buttons and buttonholes, or a small ruffle along the top placket, or even pocket flaps.

… using contrasting fabrics in plackets, cuffs, collar, or under collar. White collars and cuffs make blue and white stripes pop and floral shirts with stripes or gingham contrast on the inside of plackets, collar stands, and cuffs provide appealing details.

… sewing a plaid or striped fabric (gingham works particularly well), and cut the plackets and cuffs on the bias grainline.

How to Style

Take a cue from Carolina Herrera and you'll never go wrong! Her chic white shirts are a part of her daily attire and are styled with a variety of wardrobe elements.

* Combine a long, white shirt with leggings and booties.

* Pair a white button-up with trousers, long skirts for evening, and short skirts for daytime. It goes with everything!

* Open necklines with a turned-up collar to elongate the neck.

* For cocktails, pair a crisp shirt with slim trousers and heels. Turn up the cuffs and leave that last button unbuttoned!

- Make your black suit pop with a white shirt. Fold the cuffs over the jacket sleeve.

- Wear your classic shirts unbuttoned over a cami and tie at the waist. This style works great with jeans or midi skirts.

- For the ultimate preppy look, wear your button-up under a sweater, letting the collar, sleeves, and bottom peak out.

- A lace shirt with satin-covered buttons and paired with a camisole has casual chic glamour.

Who Wore It

We give credit to women everywhere with rocking the classic white shirt, but we certainly have a few favorite and famous "white shirt moments."

MARILYN MONROE in *The Misfits* · LAUREN BACALL in *Key Largo* · GRACE KELLY in *High Noon*

DIANE KEATON in *Annie Hall* · JENNIFER GREY in *Dirty Dancing* · JULIA ROBERTS in *Pretty Woman*

AUDREY HEPBURN in *Breakfast at Tiffany's* · UMA THURMAN in *Pulp Fiction*

EMMA WATSON when she dined with royalty at Windsor Castle in 2014

MARLENE DIETRICH in *Morocco* · KATHARINE HEPBURN in *Desk Set*

The T-Shirt

Everyone has a favorite T-shirt or two. Whether it's a sentimental treasure or one with the perfect fit, the simple shape and easy fit of the T-shirt make it a long-lasting closet staple we can't live without.

"Style; all who have it have one thing: originality." DIANA VREELAND

History

Hello, Marlon Brando. The year was 1951 and the movie was *A Streetcar Named Desire*. The humble work-wear staple that he wore suddenly got sexy, and annual T-shirt sales exploded to $180 million.

The original T-shirt, first issued to U.S. Navy submariners to provide relief from their itchy wool uniforms, eventually became the unofficial uniform of the working man. After its Hollywood debut, the journey of the white T-shirt spanned cultures, sexes, classes, and styles before landing as an essential fashion staple for both men and women.

In 1991 Karl Lagerfeld demonstrated the genius of both his creativity and the iconic garment by pairing Chanel tweed cardigan jackets over white T-shirts for the hip-hop inspired fall collection.

As the T-shirt expanded from workwear into classic wardrobe pieces, designers and manufacturers experimented with fabrics beyond the original white cotton jersey. In addition, to new neckline variations, polyester, silk, rayon and linen knits, along with cotton jersey continue to bring different personalities to each garment. Today's factory manufactured T-shirts are often produced on a circular loom which eliminates the side seams, but don't let this stop you from making one of these easy to sew classics! Side seams or even a center back seam provide greater control for a perfect fit.

Characteristics

This casual garment is named after the T-shape of its body and sleeves. Men's and women's T-shirts are designed to fit differently. The classic women's T-shirt is fitted at the shoulders with a hemline ending below the belt but above the crotch. The sleeve hem of classic tees ends just above the bicep. *Slim-fit* T-shirts lay close to the body, hugging a woman's curves, while the *relaxed-fit* versions feature a looser, but *never* boxy fit! The original T-shirt featured a crew neckline sewn with a ribbed knit neckband, but today's T-shirt necklines include V-necks, scoop necks, cowl-necks, or bateau necklines. T-shirts are always sewn from knits!

Sewing Tips

- If your fabric is washable, preshrink it—twice. If the fabric is not machine washable, be certain to have it dry cleaned before garment construction.

- Follow the stretch guide on your pattern since different patterns might be designed for different types of stretch fabrics. Likewise, if you are duplicating a ready-to-wear garment, test the stretch for consistency in the garment and in the fabric.

- If you're seeking a casual shirt, a ribbed knit band is an ideal neckline and sleeve finish. A nonribbed knit works too, but note that it is less likely to have the same amount of stretch as ribbing.

- After folding the neck edge crosswise, baste the raw edges together to prevent shifting.

- Stabilize shoulder seams with tricot interfacing or stay tape before sewing the front and back together.

- Look for online classes (see Resources: Related Articles, Videos, and Online Classes, page 174) for invaluable tips in perfecting and refining your T-shirt making skills.

- Consider both your fabric and pattern design before cutting. Side seams offer more control with fit over a single back seam, but they may distract from the simplicity of the garment. It's your call!

Fabric Suggestions

T-shirts are typically sewn from lightweight knits such as cotton jersey, including pima and slub jersey, silk jersey, polyester jersey, stretch lace, rayon knit, linen knit, and interlock. Exceptions can include sequin mesh due to its light weight and stretch.

Think beyond solid colors when sewing these easy shirts! Stripes, animal prints, camo prints, and bold prints are ideal for a quick wardrobe refresher!

Design Variations

There are countless ways to embellish and change the shape of your T-shirts. Enjoy the creative process to make them your own.

• Bring a girly touch to your T-shirt with tassel or pom-pom trim sewn on the hemline and/or sleeves. Or, try embellishing the front of the T-shirt with strategically placed lace inserts.

• Try contrasting ribbed knits for the sleeve bands and neckline; metallic ribbing on white, or striped ribbing for a "Gucci" look. High-end designers often trim a solid white T-shirt with a signature logo knit trim. Always be on the lookout for trims to put a unique stamp on your T-shirt.

• While most T-shirts feature the traditional fitted shoulders, raglan sleeves in contrasting colors offer a sporty variation.

How to Style

T-shirts are casual. Although we've seen them paired with every imaginable garment, they are by nature designed for informal and relaxed dressing. It takes a woman with a certain *je ne sais quoi* to pull off wearing a T-shirt with a ball gown, but it can be done. Try wearing it …

… with a blazer and jeans.

… with jeans and sneakers.

… with jeans, ballet flats, and a cardigan.

… as a sequined tee to holiday cocktail parties paired with black skinny pants.

… in black with a black leather jacket and boots for biker chic.

… under a poncho; it's perfect for a cold flight to a warm climate.

… with your favorite denim jacket and short skirt.

… with a French jacket in a complementary color to take the jacket down a notch, and complete the look with your favorite white or dark jeans and pumps.

Who Wore It

Lots of people have worn the T-shirt, but these personalities are sexy standouts!

BRUCE SPRINGSTEEN · MADONNA · BROOKE SHIELDS · JAMES DEAN · BRIGITTE BARDOT
CALVIN KLEIN · GIORGIO ARMANI · SHARON STONE · KENDALL JENNER · REESE WITHERSPOON

Turtleneck

This little gem is the unsung hero of a stylish wardrobe! The turtleneck is not only warm but it possesses a figure-flattering silhouette. Whether worn as a top or as a dress, sleeveless, short or long sleeved, this classic garment is a practical wardrobe staple that can hold its own or serve as a layering piece.

"Behold the turtle. He makes progress only when he sticks his neck out." JAMES BRYANT CONANT

History

The saying goes: *The sweater girls made it sexy, but Audrey Hepburn made it timeless.*

As a staple in nineteenth-century workwear and as part of the U.S. Navy WWII uniform, the humble turtleneck eventually found its home with the beatnik scene before Audrey Hepburn elevated its status to a timeless classic in her memorable *Funny Face* dancing scene.

Characteristics

The classic turtleneck sweater is sewn from knit fabrics. It features a high and close-fitting collar.

Sewing Tips

- Sewing the turtleneck is not difficult! The collar is stretched to the neckline to produce a snug fit around the neck; therefore, it requires fabrics with a generous horizontal stretch. Fitted turtlenecks often feature negative ease, making the stretch factor most important.

- Loosely woven knits should be staystitched at the neckline and armscye immediately upon cutting to prevent stretching.

- The beauty of sewing is the ability to make a garment work for you! If your turtleneck collar is too long for your neck, simply adjust the length of the pattern piece.

- To avoid bulk, sew the back seam of the turtleneck on your sewing machine rather than the serger and press the seam open before folding and attaching it to the bodice.

- Turtleneck sweaters without a lower hem band are more versatile than those sewn with a lower band. If your pattern features a lower band that you wish to omit, be sure to add length back to the front and back bodice patterns.

- Twin needles produce lovely topstitching, and tear-away stabilizer is often used underneath the fabric during the sewing process to prevent buckling.

Fabric Suggestions

As previously mentioned, turtlenecks require fabric with a generous horizontal stretch. Rib knits, jerseys, cotton knits, bamboo knits, sweater knits, stretch velvet, and cashmere produce fabulous turtlenecks. Although traditional turtlenecks are solid-color long-sleeve garments, think outside the box when sewing this garment!

Design Variations

Variations include the cold shoulder, short sleeves, or even sleeveless sweaters with cut-in shoulders. Consider turning your favorite turtleneck into a form-fitting dress by extending the pattern a few inches to your desired dress length. And, most certainly go trendy with a cropped turtleneck sewn in a large cable knit or similar heavier fabric.

How to Style

- Capture the nautical spirit by pairing a navy turtleneck with wide-legged white pants.

- Turtlenecks are perfect layering pieces! Wear underneath blazers, jeans jackets, cardigans, and boyfriend shirts.

- Accessorize with scarves for added texture.

- Channel your inner Audrey Hepburn by wearing a black turtleneck with slim black cigarette pants and ballet flats.

- It's all about proportions! Balancing the volume of a chunky turtleneck with slim jeans, leggings, or a pencil skirt will provide a flattering silhouette and eliminate the common pitfall associated with the baggy look—added pounds!

Who Wore It

Some people can make anything look cool!

STEVE JOBS • AUDREY HEPBURN
KIM KARDASHIAN • MARILYN MONROE
KATE MOSS • ROBERT REDFORD • ANDY WARHOL
DEBBIE HARRY • PRINCESS DIANA • THE BEATLES

Bateau Neckline

According to Clare Waight Keller of Givenchy, designer of Meghan Markle's classically simple bateau neckline wedding gown, the graphic open neck gracefully frames the shoulders and balances the midsection by drawing the eye outward. Whether worn by sailors, movie stars, or modern-day royalty, it's a modest but modern look that imparts a composed and informal cool. The "bateau" is now an enduring icon for women and men alike.

"Elegance is not standing out, but being remembered" GIORGIO ARMANI

History

Ahoy, mates! The bateau neckline or boat neck, originally called a marinière or Breton shirt, was introduced as the uniform of sailors in the French Navy in 1858 when the horizontal blue stripes on a white ground were said to help spot men who had fallen overboard. Coco Chanel took notice of their snappy stripes during her seaside holidays during World War I, and incorporated the nautical style into her 1917 collection using a simple jersey fabric. Leaving behind the stiff girdles of the day, Chanel adopted her own casual "garçonne style" into jersey sportswear. Women said, "Yes, please!" and the bateau neckline rose quickly into a fashion staple. The 1950's and 60's French cinema readopted the sailor look and soon Hollywood hopped on board. Today you're as sure to find a bateau neckline garment in fashionable wardrobes as a baguette in a *boulangerie*!

Characteristics

A bateau shirt or dress features a wide neckline that runs horizontally, front and back, almost to the shoulder points, and grazes the collarbone. The bodice is the same height in the front as in the back and should lay flat against the chest without dipping or gaping.

Sewing Tips

* This neckline can be finished with knit binding (exposed or turned under), bias tape, a facing, or a quick easy hem (with a finished raw edge that has been turned and stitched).

* The simplest versions are made by adding neck binding to the raw edges before joining the shoulder seams. For a tidier appearance, apply the neck binding after the front and back have been assembled.

* Fusible interfacing is a great aid in stabilizing the corners and preventing your neckline from stretching. If you prefer the clean look and additional structure of a secure facing, consider choosing a pattern which includes a wide facing that is sewn into the armscye seam. When using woven fabrics, your bateau must include a facing and an opening in the back of the garment. The back opening consists of either a faced keyhole or slit with button or hook at the back neck or sometimes a zipper.

Fabric Suggestions

Striped knits are the obvious choice for effortless French flair. However, bateau neckline daytime dresses, cocktail attire, and eveningwear in a wide variety of fabrics including crepe knits, lace, and brocade are suddenly everywhere since the Duchess of Sussex adopted it as her signature style. In fact, the "Meghan Markle effect" is thought to have accounted for an 80% uptick in eBay searches for the style.

How to Style

* The classic blue-and-white–stripe bateau neckline shirt with a pair of white jeans is one of our favorite never-fail outfits.

* Add a few brass buttons to each shoulder for a fun nautical touch.

* For cooler weather, try a bateau neckline sweater over a white shirt with slim pants and ballet flats. Or perhaps add a small silk neckerchief knotted at the throat for a bit of Parisian whimsy.

- Coco Chanel preferred her bateau with long flared trousers.

- Dresses in every cut from casual jersey knit pullovers to fit and flare party dresses work well in this low-key but subtly sexy style.

- You might want to consider finishing the front and back neckline edges with a scalloped edge, using a scallop template and a facing for a soft, romantic detail.

- Proportionally speaking, short necklaces distract and compete with the horizontal line of a bateau neckline, so it's best to select longer necklaces and pendants.

Who Wore It

Enjoy a little seaside sass wherever you may be—you need not be French to wear the bateau!

COCO CHANEL
PABLO PICASSO
MARCEL MARCEAU
AUDREY HEPBURN
BRIGITTE BARDOT
JAMES DEAN
LEE MARVIN
CARY GRANT
JOHN WAYNE
MARY TYLER MOORE
MEGHAN MARKLE

Tunic

From the Roman Empire to the fashion runways, the functional and fashionable tunic has maintained its appeal for thousands of years. Extremely versatile, classic tunics are considered both elegant and modern. Their loose fit allows you to move freely and stay cool. Sew one, or many, for easy dressing!

"The tunic is the new white shirt."

MICHAEL KORS

History

Our love of tunics led us to write our first book, *The Tunic Bible* (page 176). The tunic, considered by historians as the original garment, follows the development of humankind from the ancient Egyptians to New York Fashion Week! Born as a simple rectangle with a center hole, the tunic became the primary garment for millions of men and women living in those early civilizations. Roman tunics featured bands of different widths, colors, and ornamentation, which identified class and status. In the Middle Ages, tunics were elaborately embellished with gold threads and braids. The simplicity of the tunic proved a perfect platform for showcasing developing textile skills, leading the garment to fulfill numerous fashion, religious, and military purposes. Today's proportions may have changed, but the word "tunic" still describes a pullover garment that mimics the silhouette of the classic Roman garment.

The *boho chic* style of fashion has wound its way through modern history, reappearing as the beatnik style and hippie culture of the 1960s, and finally, to the resortwear styles of today by designers worldwide.

Characteristics

A tunic is an extended mid-thigh or longer over-blouse of any style, usually straight or slightly fitted and worn beltless. Although the tunic bodice remains consistent, changing a single detail, such as the neckline, placket, trim, or collar, often affects a tunic's entire appearance. Whether decorative or functional, the neckline frames the face and distinguishes the overall style of a tunic. Sleeves make a powerful statement about your garment, whether trimmed, tailored, or whimsical. A simple change of sleeve style can transform the personality of your tunic.

Sewing Tips

• Tunics can be as simple or as elaborate as you choose. Whether your style is everyday casual, preppy chic, bohemian, or glamorous, creating the ideal tunic for your lifestyle is easy for anyone who sews! Many of our favorite ready-to-wear tunics are shaped from the back with two contoured back darts. Heavier fabrics and longer lengths often require more structure for a flattering fit. An invisible side zipper is recommended for fitted tunics sewn in nonstretch fabrics.

• Embellishing your tunic is where the fun begins. Ribbons and trim add richness and variety, resulting in the sought-after ready-to-wear look. Even very simple trims bring extraordinary beauty through added dimension. Our favorite trims include twill tape, Petersham and woven ribbon, braid, open cording, beaded appliqués, and novelty offerings.

Fabric Suggestions

LINEN FABRICS

Embrace those wrinkles! Natural linen looks best when it's beautifully rumpled. Linen tunics exist in every color combination imaginable, from tone-on-tone to stark contrasts and digital prints.

COTTON FABRICS

Versatile, breathable, low-maintenance, and affordable, all types of cotton fabrics are a perennial favorite for tunic construction.

SILK FABRICS

Silk fabrics such as twill, dupioni, crepe de chine, and charmeuse produce gorgeous results. Whether your goal is to dress up your jeans or make a gala-worthy tunic, look no further than silk! Once considered an extravagance and reserved for royalty, silk is now widely available in a variety of price ranges. Don't shy away from sewing silk—while it looks and feels delicate, many silks are strong and easy to sew.

KNITS

Easy to dress up or down with a change of accessories, a knit tunic is a welcome travel companion. Today, nearly every fiber is available in a knit form! We identify knits according to the following categories: stable knits, midweight knits, and lightweight knits. All provide ravishing results!

How to Style

• The key to successful tunic styling is knowing how to balance its volume. Tunics look best with a slim bottom.

• The hip-length tunic is a great choice to pair with leggings, skinny jeans, shorts, and Capris. It should end just above or below the widest area of your body.

• The all-occasion dress length tunic opens a world of one-piece dressing possibilities. Dress and go!

• Paired with flip-flops, the ankle-grazing maxi length tunic brings a fresh approach to street-style dressing. A summer staple, the maxi is always a great option for looking hot while staying cool.

• Take a maxi-length tunic out on the town in silky fabrics and heels.

Who Wore It

Whether in boho or resort mode, these stylish adventurers enjoyed wearing free-spirited tunic designs.

TALITHA GETTY · LILLY PULITZER · TORY BURCH · GRETCHEN SCOTT · OPRAH WINFREY · MARYAM MONTAGUE
MEGHAN MARKLE · THE BEATLES

Cardigan Sweater

Mr. Roger's red cardigan is displayed in the Smithsonian Museum. This iconic classic represents his cherished personality traits of warmth, coziness, and reliability. While this practical garment continues to evolve and change each year, its underlying spirit remains the same.

"I always wear my sweater back to front. It's so much more flattering." DIANA VREELAND

History

After James Brudenell, the 7th Earl of Cardigan and a British Army Major General, led the Charge of the Light Brigade at the Battle of Balaclava during the Crimean War, his fame soared and so did his garment—a knitted wool waistcoat with missing tails that had accidentally burned off in a fireplace. He liked it that way and the cardigan sweater was born. However, it was Coco Chanel who popularized cardigans for women because she disliked how tight-necked sweaters messed up her hair when she pulled them over her head.

Since the Roaring Twenties, the cardigan sweater has appealed to both men and women. Oversized hip-length sweaters prevailed as the sports team letter sweaters swarmed high schools throughout the 50s. Teenage women coveted their steady beaus' athletic sweaters, which inspired the later cross-dressing fad of the boyfriend look.

Characteristics

Traditionally made of wool, the classic cardigan has an open front that is closed with buttons. Today, many cardigans feature a V-neck or scoop neckline and are offered in a variety of fabrics, with button or zip-front closures, or no closure at all. Shapes vary from boxy to the more fitted twinset silhouette.

Sewing Tips

• Always compare your fabric's stretch to the stretch chart on the pattern envelope.

• After cutting out each pattern piece, it is imperative to staystitch around all the cut edges that might stretch during stitching. This step will help your knit fabrics maintain their shape.

• Stabilize shoulder seams with stay tape or clear elastic.

• Use a stretch sewing machine needle to prevent damaging the fabric.

• Cut larger seam allowances for loose knits (larger gauge) to allow for potential raveling.

Fabric Suggestions

Knit fabrics abound, particularly online. When planning a cardigan sewing project, consider cashmere, cable knit, ribbed knits, sweater knit, merino wool, cotton knits, wool jersey, mohair, and novelty knits.

Design Variations

From fitted sweater set cardigans to sweater coats, the cardigan sweater is customizable to suit your taste and needs. Fine-gauge cropped cardis, long waterfall cardigans, cable knits with leather buttons, and zippered boxy sweaters are easy sewing projects.

How to Style

• The larger the sweater the slimmer the bottom. Oversize cardigans paired with slim jeans provide a flattering proportional balance. Try a camel-hued cardigan with black skinny jeans and leopard accents.

• Wear your fitted cardigan with fit and flare dresses or high-waisted skirts.

• Heathered cardigans work well with denim.

• Enjoy long cardigans, turtlenecks, skinny jeans and boots during fall and winter weather.

• Fitted cardigans (not too tight!) over tailored pants bring an edgy factor to office dressing.

Who Wore It

DIANA VREELAND · ANNA WINTOUR
FRED ROGERS · MEG RYAN · MICHELLE OBAMA
LANA TURNER in *They Won't Forget*
C. Z. GUEST · AUDREY HEPBURN
GRACE KELLY

Twin Sweater Set

Who would have thought a simple sweater set could be considered trouble by some, and elegant by others? From *bombshells* to *bobby-soxers*, the sweater set was all the rage during the 50s. Viewed with alarm for its tight fit before becoming the elegant twinset of memorable Hollywood films, the cardigan and crew neck sweater set has found its place among the classics.

"I like my clothes tight enough to show I'm a woman, but loose enough to show I'm a lady." EDITH HEAD

History

The twin sweater set made its inaugural appearance in the 1930s, thanks to sweater manufacturer Pringle of Scotland, inspired by sporty styles worn on golf courses.

Early twinsets were associated most often with stenographers and schoolmarms and are still used by directors and costume designers in the modern film industry when a character portrayal calls for conservatism or frumpiness. However, there was nothing frumpy about the chic cashmere twinsets which regularly graced the shoulders of such Hollywood luminaries as Lana Turner, Joan Fontaine, Jane Russell, and Joan Crawford. Their snug, form fitting twinsets provocatively emphasized the bust line and the catchphrase "sweater girls" was coined to maximize the impact of their sex appeal.

Characteristics

Twinsets consist of a long-sleeved, button-front cardigan sweater over a matching sleeveless shell or short sleeved, round crew neck pullover. A row of small decorative pearl, shell, or jeweled buttons add luster or sparkle.

Sewing Tips

- To sew a perfectly smooth and evenly distributed neck-band on the shell, use the shoulder seams as quarter points and mark the center front and center back on the neckband. Stretch only the neckband as you sew, and not the front and back sweater pieces.

- Make the buttonholes prior to attaching the center front bands to avoid seamline interference and guarantee consistently spaced and smooth finishes.

Fabric Suggestions

Identical fabrics most often come to mind, but knits with repeated elements such as borders, and patterns such as argyle, can also lend cohesive harmony. Cashmere is the gold standard, but silk jersey, angora, rayon, or any fine-gauge knit makes an elegantly coordinated impression.

How to Style

- Pull out your pearls! The twinset is the ideal backdrop to feature a strand (or two or three!), statement jewelry, or a special brooch.

- Pair it with a tweed or tartan skirt and a little silk scarf tied around the neck for an understated fashion statement that quietly speaks volumes.

Who Wore It

JOAN FONTAINE in *Rebecca*

LANA TURNER in *They Won't Forget*

GRACE KELLY in *Rear Window*

PIPPA MIDDLETON at Wimbledon

SCARLETT JOHANSSON in *The Black Dahlia*

MEG RYAN in *You've Got Mail*

GWYNETH PALTROW at the 1999 Golden Globes

MICHELLE OBAMA when she met Queen Elizabeth

Dresses

Shift Dress

Always comfortable and always fresh, the classic shift is easy to style and easy to wear. Its simple, clean lines beautifully showcase multiple types of fabrics and designs. Count on this classic to remain a go-to garment for women of all ages, in all places!

"Life is a party—dress like it!" LILLY PULITZER

History

Think freedom! That's exactly what inspired the short flapper dresses of the 1920s. No more restrictions, no more corsets, and lots of freedom to move, dance, and party the night away. The shift was a cultural statement as well as a fashion trend rebelling against the restrictive Victorian lifestyle, but it was not until the 1960s when the modern-day shift emerged as a permanent fixture in the fashion world.

During the 60s, Mary Quant featured the shift as a minidress; Lilly Pulitzer made millions from her business, which she began with a floral shift, created to hide juice stains while working at her family's fruit stand; and Yves Saint Laurent created the graphic Mondrian shift. Designers around the world continue to put their spin on this classic dress.

Characteristics

The classic shift silhouette was introduced as a sleeveless straight dress, fitted at the shoulders with no waistline definition. Bearing a high scoop neckline, the bust is typically fitted with darts and the dress skims the hips. The length typically varies from mini to knee length.

Sewing Tips

• What tips can we provide for sewing such an easy garment? More than sewing this garment, the work is in properly cutting out the pattern pieces. No matter whether you decide to cut the patterns on the lengthwise, crosswise, or even on the bias grainline of the fabric, your pattern pieces *must* be placed and cut perfectly on or against the fabric's grain. If not, the shift will hang improperly.

• If you are sewing with patterned fabric, place your pattern pieces carefully. Geometrics should be centered within the patterns and plaids should match at the seams.

• Before cutting out your fabric, consider how darts, once stitched, affect your fabric design. Small busted women also have the option of removing the darts. (See Resources: Related Articles, Videos, and Online Classes, for Maria Denmark, page 174.)

• You can never go wrong sewing a muslin before cutting into your fashion fabric! Sewing patterns are designed for standardized measurements and many sewists require alterations for a perfect fit. If the pattern waistline is lower than your waistline, the shift will not fit over the hips! (See The Importance of Sewing a Muslin, page 55.)

• The need to add lining to the shift depends on your fabric. While it's not a requirement, a lining makes most garments more comfortable, more durable, substantial, and less prone to wrinkles!

• In this era of the sleeve, the shift silhouette is perfect for showcasing the statement sleeve of your choice. Try using a sleeve from a different pattern with a similar armscye circumference.

• Have fun embellishing your shift with many types of trims! Gold trims centered down the front elevate any fabric to cocktail status; lace trims on bright florals produce the Lilly Pulitzer look. Pom-pom trim around the hemline adds a whimsical touch, while piped seams create a preppy chic appeal.

Fabric Suggestions

Modern, tropical, classic, avant garde ... any look is achievable with the shift. Cotton, cotton blends, stable knits, poplins, crepes, silks, piqués, bouclés, lightweight tweeds, and sequined fabrics all work nicely with the shift silhouette. The shift is your chance to creatively express your style! Consider using border and graphic prints, color blocking, geometrics, and bold florals!

How to Style

* This is the perfect time to pull out your bold sunglasses!

* Style solid-color shifts with bold statement jewelry and architectural-style sandals.

* Bold graphic shifts need little more than compatible shoes to complete the look.

* Add a denim jacket and a lightweight scarf for versatile, layered weekendwear.

* Pair this dress with tights and boots for mod winter styling.

* For warm-weather, casual dressing, team your shifts with chic summer hats, stylish sneakers, and sandals.

Who Wore It

This is one garment that goes with the flow ... as these fashion icons have proven!

AUDREY HEPBURN • MIA FARROW • TWIGGY
JACQUELINE KENNEDY • GRACE KELLY
LILLY PULITZER

The Importance of Sewing a Muslin

Don't risk ruining your good fashion fabric. The the time to sew a muslin!

Fit is a crucial element to successful sewing, and, just as for ready-to-wear clothing, sewing patterns are designed for specific shapes and sizes. Rarely do we sew a new pattern without first sewing a simple muslin.

Making a muslin—or a *toile*, as it is also referred to—eliminates potential technical issues and provides an opportunity to perfect your fit. Prewashed, inexpensive muslin fabric is all you need for most woven fabric projects. When making a muslin for knit garments, choose fabrics with a similar stretch quality as your fashion fabric. Later we refer to sewing a muslin for a sheath dress; however, the practice of sewing a muslin applies to all garment types. (See Resources: Related Articles, Videos, and Online Classes, page 174.)

Cut muslin pieces for the garment front, garment back, and one sleeve, unless there are unique pattern pieces integral to the garment fit. Mark the grainlines, waistline, and darts directly on the muslin. Sew the darts and main garment seams, and insert one sleeve. Installing the zipper will provide a truer fit of the pattern.

While wearing the appropriate undergarments, try on the muslin and assess the fit in a full-length mirror. This is the time to make sure you like the look of the garment from all angles. Taking photographs is a helpful aid. For more complete fitting and alteration resources, see Resources: Sewing Instruction and Alteration Books (page 175).

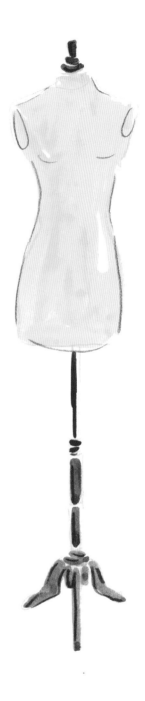

Sheath Dress

Think of the sheath as your CCC dress—church, cocktails, and cemetery dress! A versatile garment that quickly transitions from daytime to evening, this classic's universal appeal caters to women of varying shapes and sizes. The sheath's streamlined simplicity lends itself to several fabrics and accessories from which endless looks are achieved. No matter the setting, a sheath is always appropriate!

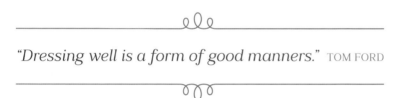

"Dressing well is a form of good manners." TOM FORD

History

Commonly seen in ancient Egyptian art, the sheath has deep roots, but it was Christian Dior who popularized the present-day sheath in the 1950s by introducing "the vertical line" to the fashion scene. In 1961, Audrey Hepburn brought Herbert Givenchy's black sheath to iconic status in *Breakfast at Tiffany's*, and the little black dress was born.

Pattern companies began producing sheaths in multiple sizes, and due to the sheath's easy assembly, it became a favorite sewing pattern.

Characteristics

The sheath is a close-fitting dress with a defined waist, typically accentuated with darts. It is often sleeveless and knee length. The one-piece sheath is fitted with either French darts or a combination of bust and long front and back darts. The two-piece sheath has a waist seam and the bodice darts meet the skirt darts at the waist so they appear as a single dart. Since the dress features a fitted skirt, garments knee length and longer feature a back slit or pleat to keep them walkable.

Sewing Tips

• The key to sewing a flattering sheath is proper fit. Make a muslin (see The Importance of Sewing a Muslin, page 55) to get your fit just right through the bodice. Adjusting the length of the bodice in a two-piece sheath by a single inch can make the difference between success and failure.

• Bust darts should point at the apex of your bust. Pressing your darts over a tailor's ham once they are sewn is crucial before moving to the next step.

• Sheaths are best lined to prevent wrinkling. Try using power mesh as lining for a subtle form of shapewear.

• Unless you are using a statement zipper, we recommend an invisible zipper to avoid distracting from the minimalistic silhouette.

Fabric Suggestions

Wool crepe, polyester crepe, bouclé, ponte knit, linen, gabardine, piqué, and stretch cottons are excellent fabric choices and work well for sheaths. Avoid clingy, lightweight fabrics as well as stiff and heavy fabrics that don't shape easily to the contours of the body.

While many sheaths are sewn in solid colors, patterned fabric will help distract attention from a specific problem area. If you can pull off bold horizontal stripes, then go for it! Horizontal stripes, not affected by vertical darts, make quite the statement.

Design Variations

The simple silhouette of the sheath allows you to easily vary the neckline. The traditional sheath features a round neckline, but consider an asymmetrical neckline for a contemporary twist, or embellishing the neckline with decorative beading. Scoop and bateau necklines add a feminine aesthetic while a front and back square neckline spells summer loud and clear. Try illusion necklines for holiday and black-tie dressing!

How to Style

• Wear your sheath on its own with a great pair of heels.

• Who can resist the *Breakfast at Tiffany's* look? A sleeveless black sheath, black pumps, and a strand of pearls is all it takes!

• For a trendier approach, accessorize your sheath with tassel earrings and chunky heels.

• For the office, pair this garment with a fitted cardigan or with a tailored or cropped jacket.

• Remember that heels continue the garment's vertical line. They need not be high!

Who Wore It

The beauty of the sheath is its versatility. One dress can easily transition into several different looks.

AUDREY HEPBURN

MARILYN MONROE

NANCY REAGAN

ROBIN WRIGHT in *House of Cards*

PRINCESS DIANA

SARAH JESSICA PARKER
in *Sex and the City*

ANNA WINTOUR

AMAL CLOONEY

ANGELINA JOLIE

A-Line and Trapeze Dresses

Due to their effortless silhouettes and flat-tering fits, the classic trapeze and A-line dresses have secured a permanent space in department stores across the globe. Both styles are especially becoming on a pear-shaped body, with the trapeze dress being a perfect silhouette for those seek-ing to camouflage a tummy. Thank you, Christian Dior and Yves Saint Laurent!

Trapeze, Please: The Hottest Cut To Flatter Any Body!" ELLE MAGAZINE

History

THE A-LINE DRESS

As with the A-line skirt, the A-line dress takes us back to Christian Dior's groundbreaking 1955 spring collection. Each of Dior's collections followed a theme bearing a descriptive title. The collections of 1954 and 1955 were named H, Y, and A. The 1955 "A" collection was a departure from the nipped in waistlines of former collections and it introduced the A-line silhouette, featuring an undefined waist and smooth silhouette that widened over the hips and legs. The less-prominent waist created a casual look, and served as a driving force through competitive fashion houses. The look was not only clean and modern, but flattering to every shape and size.

THE TRAPEZE DRESS

Following Christian Dior's death in 1957, 21-year-old Yves Saint Laurent (YSL) was named the head designer at the House of Dior. The following year, YSL took the A-line collection a step further by introducing the trapeze dress. This dress marked the beginning of his international stardom. Designers worldwide embraced the A-line and trapeze dress silhouettes, but the mod London fashion scene catapulted both styles from the fashion houses to the forefront of streetwear in mini dresses modeled by famed London models of the 1960s.

Characteristics

Easy fitting, and easy-to-sew, A-line and trapeze dresses are fitted at the shoulders and generally feature back closures of zippers or keyhole cutouts. The trapeze dress tends to be more free-flowing than the A-line, with a hemline that moves when you do.

THE A-LINE DRESS

Fitted from the shoulder to the hips, the traditional A-line dress is more streamlined than the trapeze silhouette and gradually widens towards the hem to create a triangular shape. Due to its simple style, the silhouette is easily customized. Common variations include color blocking or a separate upper bodice attached to a skirt, creating an empire seamline. From mini to maxi, the A-line is adaptable to every length!

THE TRAPEZE DRESS

The shape of the trapeze dress—and its name—are inspired by the trapezoid. The dress features a cut that is fitted through the neckline and shoulders before flaring out into a tentlike shape. The unstructured silhouette is designed to gracefully swing with the slightest movement. With a hem falling just below the knee, YSL's modern dress was designed to be worn with low-heel shoes and was considered quite youthful.

Sewing Tips

Although the A-line and trapeze dresses are safe choices for sewists without advanced skills, the fit and construction should be impeccable! Making a muslin helps hone the little details to provide an enviable fit (see The Importance of Sewing a Muslin, page 55). Always check the shoulder fit and bust dart placements and adjust as needed.

THE A-LINE

- Even with a relaxed fit, the waistline pattern marking should coincide with your natural waistline, otherwise the skirt proportion and zipper placement will appear unbalanced.

- Your muslin will indicate whether the sweep of the skirt is proportionally correct for your height and body shape. A petite sewist may wish to reduce the skirt sweep to avoid being dwarfed, while an extremely tall woman might desire a slightly larger flare. This adjustment is made by adjusting the side seam angle, since the front is cut on the fold.

- Heavier weight fabrics do not require a lining, so it is important to clean finish the seam allowances. Make sure to press as you stitch so if there are crossing seams (as for color blocked dresses) the seam allowances are pressed open before they are attached to other fabric pieces.

- Should you decide to line your A-line, we recommend lightweight linings such as Bemberg rayon, cotton batiste, and silk, otherwise the dress will be too heavy.

THE TRAPEZE

- Trapeze dress patterns feature either a back zipper or a keyhole opening at the back neckline. A thread-loop buttonhole provides a ready-to-wear finishing detail and is an excellent couture technique to master. Fortunately, learning this technique is easy and well worth the effort.

- When making these floaty garments in lightweight and sheer fabrics, we recommend using French seams for a clean finish. If you choose to line the dress, the lining should be slimmer than the actual dress. Since the dress movement can reveal the lining, you should clean finish the seams and wear the lining wrong side to the skin.

- Hem sheer fabrics with a narrow or evenly rolled hem (see Resources: Sewing Instruction and Alteration Books, page 175).

Fabric Suggestions

Like the A-line skirt, the A-line dress is suitable for midweight fabrics including wool crepe, cotton broadcloth, denim, heavier silks, lace, suede, and stable knits such as ponte and scuba knit. The A-line provides plenty of opportunity to get creative with border prints, large florals, stripes, and geometrics!

The trapeze dress is perfect for graphic prints, using lightweight and sheer fabrics such as chiffon, crepe, lightweight linen, silks, jersey, and stable knits. Linings are best sewn in lightweight fabrics such as polyester, rayon, silk, or mesh fabrics to keep the dress light and floaty.

Design Variations

A-line dress embellishments include, but aren't limited to, patch pockets, piping, color-blocking, and topstitching.

While the cut of the trapeze dress is dramatic on it's own, it easily caters to the whims of a designer! Let your imagination run wild with hemline variations such as handkerchief and asymmetrical hems, tassel hems, high-low hems, high necks, cut-in shoulders, one-shoulder ruffles, and bias-cut striped fabrics.

How to Style

Have fun with these dresses!

- The A-line dress can handle practically any accessory depending on your fabric choice and/or color-blocking.

- Treat a solid color A-line as a blank canvas. Whether you take a conservative approach with pearls and pumps or go for a 60's vibe with tights and boots, the A-line will go with the flow.

- Tropical prints worn with gold sandals or wedges embody warm-weather fun and island vacations.

- Try a plaid knee-length A-line with ankle boots for a fall weekend rendezvous with your better half.

- Be wedding guest–ready in a lace A-line with strappy sandals.

- Although anything goes these days, the trapeze dress was originally designed to be worn with low heels.

- Go bold with earrings but light with necklaces, and let the trapeze silhouette do the talking! Chandelier and tassel earrings swing with the fabric and work nicely for the evening, but put on your hoops during the day!

- The striking cut and movement of the trapeze dress brings attention your way so put yourself in a charming state of mind and enjoy the moment!

Who Wore It

A-line fashion icons include:

JACQUELINE KENNEDY • GRACE KELLY • AUDREY HEPBURN • MARLO THOMAS • DIAHANN CARROLL

Trapeze fashion icons include:

TWIGGY • JEAN SHRIMPTON • JESSICA ALBA • VICTORIA BECKHAM • DIANA ROSS

Fit and Flare Dress

Considered a universally flattering silhouette, the versatile fit and flare dress looks equally great on women of all physiques, and remains age appropriate for every stage of life. On slim figures, it creates shapely curves, while fuller figures appreciate its ability to *glide and hide*!

"I want people to see the dress, but focus on the woman." VERA WANG

History

What's a princess to do? The year was 1947 and the war had ended two years earlier. Like many British women, Princesses Elizabeth and Margaret were weary of wearing dreary utility clothing due to fabric restrictions, and were keen to update their wardrobes with the fashionably full-skirted silhouettes of Dior's "New Look." Unfortunately for the Windsor sisters, their father, King George, put his royal foot down, fearing the voluminous clothes would give the appearance of waste while fabric rationing was still in effect.

Characteristics

To create the classic fit and flare silhouette, a perfectly fitted bodice is a must! The bodice is fitted with princess seams or bust darts. Princess-seam fit and flare dresses are often designed as one-piece dresses, while bodices fitted with bust darts feature a separate skirt flared with gathers, pleats, or bias-cut shaping. Almost any neckline is suitable, including variations such as sweetheart, strapless, spaghetti straps, square necklines, and even one-shoulder bodices. Due to the dress's dramatic silhouette, sleeves variations from cap to long are kept simple.

Sewing Tips

- Waist placement is important to consider when sewing this style, since it has a big impact on balance and the overall effect. Generally, most figures should aim for the garment waistline to hit an inch above the natural waistline, which is the slimmest point of most women's midriffs. A placement slightly below the natural waist may give the graceful appearance of a lean and elongated torso. Alternately, a waistline that is too high can emphasize a larger bust.

- Hem circumference (also called *sweep*) is also an important design feature for a balanced look. Petite figures may choose to reduce the hem flare circumference. If the sweep, or flare, is too great, it can look overwhelming by visually shortening and adding width to small frames.

- Pear-shaped bodies benefit from a bateau, sweetheart, asymmetrical, or other distinctive neckline, which can balance the body and draw the eye upward. V-necklines and halter styles elongate the upper body.

- For a customized bodice fit and fewer alterations when sewing your muslin, select patterns that offer multi-cup sizing. (See The Importance of Sewing a Muslin, page 55.)

- The graceful vertical lines of princess seams lend themselves especially well to the bodice of the fit and flare dress. For perfect symmetry when sewing princess seams, staystitch just inside the seamline and clip the seam allowances to prevent puckers, ripples, or distortion in the finished dress. Carefully press the seams over a ham for better shaping.

Fabric Suggestions

A myriad of fabric options provides endless opportunities to create multiple dresses with unique personalities, from the garden party dress to the wedding guest dress and even to the sweet sixteen dress.

Cotton or blended knits lend themselves to a sporty skater-style dress; underlined eyelet makes for a romantic sundress; taffeta or brocade are perfect for party dressing; embroidered mesh overlays add an elegant touch for eveningwear and special occasions; and bouclé and tweed are perfect fabrics for officewear. Consider combining different fabrics for the bodice and skirt to create a one-piece dress that resembles separates.

How to Style

Other than a little jewelry, a fit and flare dress rarely needs excessive styling since the voluminous style speaks for itself—but for adventurous spirits:

- Try a button-up shirt under a sleeveless fit and flare dress for a layered effect.

- Add a belted blazer for a touch of office chic.

- Wear it with a cropped jacket or short cardigan to accentuate the flared skirt.

- Boots, tights, and a turtleneck turn your long sleeve ponte fit and flare into a cool-weather staple outfit.

- Follow the classic French footwear guide: If the skirt is above the knee, wear flats, chunky heels, or wedges. Longer lengths look best with heels.

Who Wore It

PHAEDRA PARKS • KATE MIDDLETON
ANNA WINTOUR • MICHELLE OBAMA
TAYLOR SWIFT • EARTHA KITT
SHIRLEY BASSEY

Wrap Dress

Can you tell the difference between a 1974 wrap dress and a current wrap dress? We can't! Easy to pack, wear, and accessorize, the wrap hugs a woman's curves without buttons or zippers. Comfort is the key element to the confidence boost instantly experienced when slipping into this classic. Its magical effect enhances your favorite body parts while camouflaging those you'd prefer to downplay.

"Feel like a woman. Wear a dress!"

DIANE VON FÜRSTENBERG

History

When Diane von Fürstenberg first skyrocketed to fame for her revolutionary wrap dress in 1974, no one was more surprised by its wild success than the designer herself. Symbolic of women's new independence and empowerment, in an instant, the wrap became forever identified with the DVF brand. Although she is widely credited with creating the style, 1930's and 1940's designers including Elsa Schiaparelli, along with Claire McCardell's "popover" designs, predated DVF's dress by decades, not to mention togas and kimonos, which wrapped the human body in ancient times.

Characteristics

A hallmark of the wrap dress is its often colorful and boldly patterned jersey fabric that wraps around the body with a crossover bodice and long ties surrounding the waist. Styles vary from mini to maxi, collared or *sans*, and long-sleeved to sleeveless. The dress is often constructed as a one-piece slim cut garment that is slightly flared or a fuller-skirted version featuring a waist seam with pleats or gathers.

Sewing Tips

Wrap dresses are as easy to sew as they are to love!

- Stabilize shoulder seams with stay tape or clear elastic.

- Be certain sleeve insertion seams are perfectly smooth, without puckers or poufs to spoil the shoulder line. One foolproof method we use is to hand baste the sleeves in flat using lots of pins.

- If modesty is a concern, consider adding a wide and decorative binding visible from the right side rather than a facing folded to the inside along the front neckline edges.

- Stitch flat elastic along the necklines to prevent gaping.

- For crisp edge finishes, apply appropriate fusible interfacing at the hemline, collar, cuffs, and ties and you will be rewarded with a dress that hugs the body smoothly and doesn't stretch out of shape. Finding the perfect combination of interfacing and fabric may require a bit of experimentation. We recommend medium-weight knit interfacings for collars and cuffs, but hems and facings can be interfaced with a lightweight interfacing.

- If your wrap has a waist seam, elastic will prevent the skirt from sagging, especially on maxi dresses where additional fabric weight may cause hems to drag.

- For a lean chic line, the most versatile and flattering length is right at the knee or slightly above.

- Use a twin needle or coverstitch machine for professional hemming results.

- Tucking hem weights (small coins are a good substitute!) or hand stitching a chain along the inside of the hem is a luxurious touch and an extra precaution to consider as insurance against windy day wardrobe malfunctions!

Fabric Suggestions

DVF's first wrap dress was made from an animal print silk jersey, which created a sleek, feline impression. But if a walk on the wild side isn't quite your style, go for feminine florals, modern geometric prints, or always-appropriate solids. Look for knits with good recovery such as silk or wool jersey, rayon or poly-spandex, and cotton knits blended with Lycra. Dress or medium-weight fabrics with good drape yield polished-looking results every time. Drape the fabric over your arm or on a dress form to get a sense of how it hangs. Stable knits such as ponte and double knits are also good options if you prefer less cling and more structure. Micro suede and sweater knits make cozy wraps for cooler weather wear.

Many wrap dress patterns are designed especially for woven fabrics. Linen, cotton sateen, piqué, and seersucker (with or without Lycra) are all options that will make cool, breathable summer dresses.

Design Variations

A faux wrap dress with surplice bodice that slips over the head is a good strategy if you prefer a bit of extra security. Wrap tops are a versatile spin on this classic and pair beautifully with all your favorite bottom pieces.

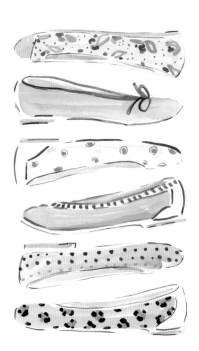

How to Style

- Don't forget shapewear to banish visible lines or bumps!

- The open neckline of the wrap bodice sets the stage for your favorite neckline, whether you wear pearls, chunky links, or stones.

- Bracelets and cuffs work especially well with 3/4-length sleeves.

- Opt for ballet flats, strappy low-heel sandals, or espadrille wedges for casual daytime wear and simple neutral pumps for the office or evenings. Too much visual distraction will compete with busy fabric prints and draw attention away from your dress.

- Booties or tall boots with tights take your wrap dress into cooler months with ease.

Who Wore It

From the Red Carpet to the White House—memorable women, memorable roles, and very memorable wrap dresses!

CYBILL SHEPHERD in *Taxi Driver* • SARAH JESSICA PARKER in *Sex and The City* • OPRAH WINFREY
at the movie premiere of *The Butler* • MERYL STREEP to accept the 2012 Academy Award for *The Iron Lady*
MICHELLE OBAMA for an official White House Christmas card • AMY ADAMS in *American Hustle*
KATE MIDDLETON, the Duchess of Cambridge, on Royal Tour in Australia

Shirtdress

The mix of a feminine silhouette with menswear detailing gives the shirtdress a distinct air of understated cool. It's the answer to every style quandary and works on many levels including workwear, eveningwear, and playtime. What could be more crisp and effortless on a summer day than a smart and stylish shirtdress?

"It's not about the dress you wear; it's about the life you lead in the dress." DIANA VREELAND

History

No husband required! The shirtdress, first presented as a feminine variation of a typical men's front-buttoned shirt, combined an attached skirt for easy one-piece dressing. No back closures meant women could quickly dress themselves without help from anyone.

World War I and World War II economic conditions made it necessary for many women to choose clothing that was practical rather than fashionable. Early 1940's versions were designed as basic utilitarian workwear featuring militaristic uniform styling due to rationing, allowing women to perform their duties with greater ease.

In 1947, Christian Dior's revolutionary "New Look" was introduced. After years of grim times and restrictions, Dior described the collection as "the return to an ideal of civilized happiness." In the

1950s, the dress became fuller and more feminine; an iconic garment that caught on around the world. Initially dubbed the shirtwaist, it was first worn with a petticoat for an exaggerated cinch-waisted hourglass look. Comfort quickly overruled and the petticoat disappeared in favor of skirts that, while still pleated and voluminous, embodied 1950's domesticity in a more casual form.

Popular TV characters of the 50s and 60s reinforced the paragon of feminine perfection by wearing the classic tailored shirtwaist, making it the outfit of choice for the typical American housewife of the era.

Characteristics

A shirtdress is, as the name suggests, a dress that borrows elements from a formal button-up shirt. The classic shirtdress customarily features a collar and a button front closing. Sleeves are historically cuffed and short- or $3/4$-length, but we're fond of sleeveless in the summer and long sleeved for cooler weather. Due to its A-line silhouette, the shirtwaist flatters nearly all body types. The style highlights the body, tends to give structure where it is needed, and balances the torso, hips, and thighs.

Sewing Tips

- Half the fun of sewing a shirtdress is mixing and matching design elements to make it your own—princess seams or darts; button bands, snaps, popover style, or placket; drawstring waist, belted, pleated, gathered, or boxy … the combinations are endless.

- Whatever you do, don't forget the pockets! June Cleaver probably used hers to tuck away a handkerchief, but we like them deep enough for our cell phone and lipstick!

- Washable wonder tape is one of our can't-live-without sewing aids, which we use to stabilize long front button bands before stitching buttonholes, and to prevent rippling prior to topstitching.

- A few drops of Fray Check left to dry on both sides of the fabric before using a chisel and hammer to cut buttonholes results in a sharp, clean opening with no ragged edges.

- Snaps are a wonderful option for those who find buttonholes a challenge.

Fabric Suggestions

You guessed it, our number one fabric choice for shirtdresses is *shirting* in cotton and linen, particularly for gathered or pleated skirt versions. Cotton fabrics such as romantic florals, embroidered seersucker, colorful African wax prints, and chambray are all good choices. Also good are silks, tencel fabric, and rayon poplin. Contrasting fabrics for plackets, bands, collars, cuffs, and facings are a fun way to add a bit of personality and a pop of color.

Midweight fabrics such as denim, corduroy, twill, and micro suede work well for shirtdresses with a boxier silhouette and a shirt tail hem. These fabrics also make great self-fabric waist sashes.

For elegant Carolina Herrera–style evening shirtdresses, consider using luxury fabrics such as lace, silk dupioni, or shantung, with glistening buttons or a jeweled belt.

How to Style

- The shirtdress can be dressed up or down; let your accessories set the tone.

- Keep things casual for easy summer style by wearing slip-on sneakers or espadrilles.

- A short denim or biker-style jacket is just the right proportion to throw on over a shirtdress.

- Give your jeans a break and take a denim shirtdress on your next vacation.

- A skinny belted cardi over a shirtdress transforms your look into a two-piece outfit.

- Try a shorter length shirtdress with Capri-length leggings and sandals or flats.

- Accent and define your waist with a fabulous statement belt.

- Wear your slim silhouette shirtdress unbuttoned, with a T-shirt underneath with skinny jeans or leggings.

Who Wore It

CAROLINA HERRERA

ELIZABETH MONTGOMERY

PATTY DUKE

PRINCESS MARGARET

TRACY REESE

TORY BURCH

DONNA REED

JUNE CLEAVER

MEGHAN MARKLE

ANNA WINTOUR

Halter Dress or Top

No matter her age or size, a woman's shoulders always look good! Bare shoulders are flirty, feminine, and flattering as well as the ideal alternative to show a little skin while avoiding a plunging neckline. In fact, the classic well-cut halter often reveals less than a tank top!

"Fashion is made by fashionable people." ROY HALSTON FROWICK

History

In 1955, Marilyn Monroe stood on a subway grate in *The Seven Year Itch* and fashion history was forever changed! Her billowing white halter neck dress set the world on fire and while she may have made the style famous, its fashion roots harken back to designers Paul Poiret in the 20s and Madeleine Vionnet in the 30s. Betty Grable's WWII-era halter neck two-piece bathing suit graced countless pinup posters. The 60's counter-culture and women's rights movements brought about the shedding of convention (along with a lot of bras!) and the halter top was symbolic of new feminist freedoms. Halston and Geoffrey Beene draped gowns of fluid matte jersey during the halter's peak of popularity in the 70's daring disco heyday (think Cher and Goldie Hawn!) This sexy classic continues to be a red-carpet favorite, creating drama and allure by today's captivating backless beauties.

Characteristics

The most recognized halter style ties behind the neck and the back is completely open, leaving the shoulders fully exposed. Its more modest cousin is the choker halter, which features a high neck, with additional coverage on the back, making it suitable for daytime, as well as evening.

Sewing Tips

- The versatility of a halter neckline cannot be overstated—you can wear this fashionable neckline for nearly every occasion.

- When cut on the bias, halters take on a stretchlike fluidity that accentuates the body's curves.

- Dress up your halter by substituting a metal collar-type necklace in place of the neck ties. Sew a seam large enough to slide the necklace through and fasten it in the back.

- When selecting a style and pattern for your halter be sure to consider proper undergarments, including convertible options and clear straps which offer the right combination of support, coverage, and discretion.

Fabric Suggestions

Knits and soft fabrics with good drape, such as silk, cotton lawn, voile, and rayon take best advantage of this body-conscious style. For a dressy look, try lined sheer fabrics or luxurious silk charmeuse gathered into a choker halter neckline that flatters with soft pleats near the face. Casual fabrics in novelty and bandana prints make fun-in-the-sun dresses (and tops), and knit fabrics are sensational for easy summer maxis.

How to Style

Modern women are rediscovering halter-neck tops and dresses for their feminine simplicity and high-style quotient.

- Stick to clean-lined silhouettes for maximum elegance and impact.

- Halter tops look as fabulous with palazzo pants for evening as they do with shorts or jeans for every day.

• A collared halter top made in a lightweight, comfortable fabric works beautifully under a close-fitting jacket for office-appropriate attire.

• A wrap (page 161) or cardigan sweater (page 45) tossed over your shoulders helps ward off evening chills or overactive restaurant AC!

Who Wore It

BETTY RUBBLE in *The Flintstones*

BETTY GRABLE on a legendary WWII pinup poster

MARILYN MONROE in *The Seven Year Itch*

CHER on *The Sonny and Cher Show*

GOLDIE HAWN on *Laugh-In*

NICOLE KIDMAN at the 2007 Academy Awards

THE
CLASSIC GARMENT
Gallery

Jeans-Style Jacket
(page 142)

Cardigan Sweater
(page 45)

Turtleneck
(page 34)

Julie (top left) • Jeans-Style Jacket, Kwik Sew 2895

Photo by William Gunn

Manju (bottom left) • Jeans-Style Jacket,
Butterick 5616

Photo by Philip Nittala / Manju Nittala

Sarah and Julie (right) • Cardigan Sweater, Helen's Closet
Blackwood Cardigan; Turtleneck, True Bias Nikko

Photo by Chris Smith

A-Line Dress
(page 59)

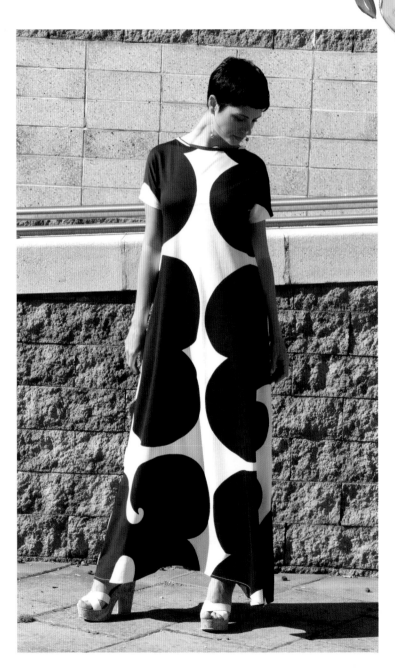

Alex • A-Line Dress, Marimekko self-drafted Maxi

Photo by Alexandra Florea

Jeans-Style Jacket

(page 142)

Sarah • Jeans-Style Jacket, McCall's 7729

Photos by William Gunn

Blazer
(page 145)

Sheath Dress
(page 56)

Sarah [top] • Blazer, Butterick 6103;
Pants, Simplicity 1665

Photo by Chris Smith

Sarah [right] • Blazer, Butterick 6103

Photo by Chris Smith

Anita [next page] • Sheath Dress, Burda 7043

Photo by Anita Morris

Trapeze Dress
(page 59)

Halter Dress
(page 73)

Tunic
(page 40)

***Sarah and Julie** [top]* • Trapeze Dress, Tessuti Ruby;
Halter Dress, Simplicity 8330
Photo by Chris Smith

***Sarah** [right]* • Tunic, *The Tunic Bible*
Photo by Chris Smith

A-Line Skirt

(page 14)

Sarah and Julie • A-Line Skirts, Burda 6904 and Annie A-Line

Photo by Chris Smith

Halter Dress
(page 73)

Shift Dress
(page 52)

Anita [top] • Halter Dress, Simplicity 1881
Photo by Anita Morris

Sarah [left] • Shift Dress (in 2 colors), New Look 6524
Photo by William Gunn

Shirtdress
(page 70)

A-Line Dress
(page 59)

Sarah [top] • Shirtdress, McCall's 6520
Photo by William Gunn

Karen [right] • A-Line Dress, Vintage Vogue 6944
Photo by Thomas B. Helm

Button-Up Shirt

(page 26)

Karon • Button-Up Shirt, Vogue 8772

Photos by Karon Cooke-Euter

Bateau Dress
(page 37)

Button-Up Jeans
Shirt (page 26) (page 122)

Julie (top) • Bateau Dress, McCall's 6571

Photo by Chris Smith

Julie (right) • Button-Up Shirt, Butterick 5526; Jeans, Jalie 2908

Photo by Chris Smith

Button-Up Shirts
(page 26)

Trench Coat
(page 149)

Julie • Button-Up Shirt, Butterick 5526

Photo by Chris Smith

Julie • Button-Up Shirt,
Sewaholic Granville

Photo by William Gunn

Lauren • Trench Coat, Sewaholic Robson Coat

Photos by Jenna Ledawn

Menswear Pajamas

(page 158)

Julie *(left)* • Menswear Pajamas, Closet Case
Carolyn Pajamas

Photo by Chris Smith

Karen *(top)* • Tunic, *The Tunic Bible*

Photo by Thomas B. Helm

Tunics
(page 40)

Andrea • Tunic, *The Tunic Bible*
Photo by Andrea Birkan

French Jacket
(page 153)

Pencil Skirt
(page 18)

Button-Up Shirt

(page 26)

Wrap Dress
(page 66)

Julie (top left) • French Jacket, Susan Khalje Couture
Classic French Jacket; Halter Top, Quick Sew 3308;
Guipure Lace Skirt, Susan Khalje Couture Classic Skirt

Photo by Chris Smith

Julie (bottom left) • Button-Up Shirt,
Rebecca Page Riviera Ruffle Shirt

Photo by William Gunn

Julie (right) • Wrap Dress, Vogue Diane Von Furstenberg 1610

Photo by Chris Smith

Jeans
(page 122)

Capri Pants
(page 135)

Lauren [top] • Jeans, Closet Case Ginger Jeans

Photos by Jenna Ledawn

Sarah [left] • T-Shirt, Grainline Pattern, Lark Tee; Capris, Simplicity 1665

Photo by William Gunn

T-Shirts ❀ Blazer
(page 30) ... *(page 145)*

Button-Up Shirt
(page 26)

Lori [top] • Blazer, McCall's 7818
Photo by Lori VanMaanen

Lori [right] • Button-Up Shirt, Grainline Archer Shirt
Photo by Lori VanMaanen

Trapeze Dress
(page 59)

Wrap Dress
(page 66)

Vatsla • Trapeze Dress, self-drafted
Photo by Vatsla Watkins

Sarah • Wrap Dress, Style Arc Leah Wrap
Photo by Chris Smith

Sheath Dress
(page 56)

A-Line Dress
(page 59)

Manju [top] • Sheath Dress, Simplicity 8292
Photo by Philip Nittala / Manju Nittala

Lucy [right] • A-Line Dress, Vogue 1809
Photo by Martin Mogaard

Button-Up Shirts
(page 26)

Sarah [top] • Button-Up Shirt, Butterick 5526

Photo by Chris Smith

Andrea [right] • Button-Up Shirt,
Sewaholic Granville Shirt

Photo by Andrea Birkan

Menswear Pajamas
(page 158)

Shift Dress (Maxi)
(page 52)

Sarah [top] • Menswear Pajamas,
Closet Case Carolyn Pajamas

Photo by William Gunn

Sarah [right] • Shift Maxi Dress, Burda 7110

Photo by William Gunn

Gored Skirt
(page 14)

Wrap
(page 161)

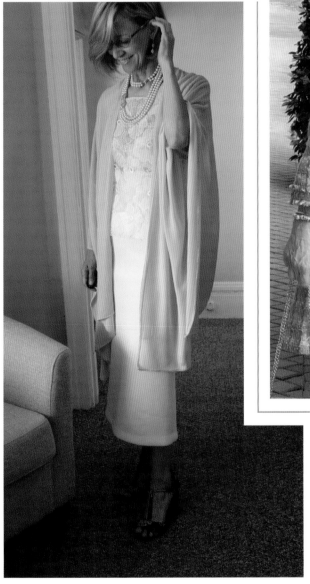

Sarah [top] • Gored Skirt, Simplicity 1560
Photo by William Gunn

Jacqueline [left] • Wrap, self-drafted
Photo by Jacqueline Foley

French Jacket

(page 153)

Button-Up  Pencil Skirt

Shirt (page 26)   (page 18)

Dorcas *[top]* • French Jacket, Vogue 7975;
Pencil Skirt, Susan Khalje Couture

Photos by Dorcas Ross

Sarah *[right]* • Pencil Skirt,
Modern Classic Pencil Skirt

Photo by William Gunn

Sheath Dress
(page 56)

Turtleneck & Pencil Skirt
(page 34)   *(page 18)*

Jacqueline *[top]* • Sheath Dress, Vogue 8630

Photo by Jacqueline Foley

Sarah *[right]* • Turtleneck, True Bias Nikko Top;
Pencil Skirt, Modern Classic Pencil Skirt

Photo by William Gunn

Tailored Trousers (Wide-Leg)

(page 128)

Wrap Dress (Top)

(page 66)

Twin Sweater Set

(page 48)

Palazzo Pants

(page 133)

French Jacket

(page 153)

Sheath Dress

(page 56)

Emily [far left] • Tailored Trousers, Vogue 8836; Wrap Top, Vogue 9319 / Vogue 9299

Photo by Emily Hallman

Julie [top] • Twin Set Cardigan, Muse Patterns Jenna Cardi; Twin Set Crew Neck, McCall's 6886; Palazzo Pants, Style Arc Sailor Sue

Photo by Chris Smith

Julie [left] • French Jacket, Susan Khalje Couture Classic French Jacket; Sheath Dress, Butterick 4386

Photo by Chris Smith

Cardigan Turtleneck
Sweater
(page 45)

(page 34)

Trench Coat
(page 149)

Sarah *[top]* • Cardigan, Helen's Closet Blackwood Cardigan; Turtleneck, True Bias, Nikko Turtleneck

Photo by Chris Smith

Lucy *[right]* • Trench Coat, Sewaholic Robson Coat

Photo by Martin Mogaard

Allie *[next page]* • Trench Coat, Deer and Doe Luzerne Trench Coat

Photo by Allie Jackson

Pencil Skirt

(page 18)

Sarah • Pencil Skirt, Modern Classic Pencil Skirt
Photo by William Gunn

Shirtdress
(page 70)

Trench Coat
(page 149)

Julie [top] • Trench Coat, Vogue 8884

Photo by William Gunn

Julie [left] • Shirtdress, Tilly and the Buttons, Rosa Shirtdress

Photo by William Gunn

Cardigan Sweater
(page 45)

Bateau Top
(page 37)

Button-Up Shirt
(page 26)

Tailored Trousers (Wide-Leg)
(page 128)

Turtleneck
(page 34)

Lori *(top)* • Turtleneck, Vogue 9275
Photo by Lori VanMaanen

Cennetta *(right)* • Button-Up Shirt, Vogue 8747;
Wide-Leg Trousers, McCall's 7445
Photo by Cennetta Burwell

Tailored Trousers (Fitted)

(page 128)

T-Shirt

(page 30)

Sarah (left) • T-Shirt, Grainline Pattern, Lark Tee; Fitted Trousers, StyleArc Elle

Photo by William Gunn

Julie (top) • Cardigan Sweater, Style Arc Nina; Bateau Top, McCall's 6571; Tailored Trousers, Closet Case Sasha Trouser

Photo by Chris Smith

Fit and Flare Dress
(page 63)

Sheath Dress
(page 56)

Birdy [top] • Fit and Flare Dress, Simplicity 1419
Photo by Duong Nguyen Lengerer

Birdy [right] • Sheath Dress, Burda Style 11-2017#121
Photos by Duong Nguyen Lengerer

Sheath Dress

(page 56)

Shift Dress

(page 52)

Sarah *(top)* • Shift Dress (in 2 colors), New Look 6524
Photos by William Gunn

Jacqueline *(left)* • Sheath Dress, Burda 6853
Photo by Jacqueline Foley

Full Skirts

(page 21)

Alex *(previous page)* • Full Skirt, Butterick 6556

Photo by Alexandra Florea

Vatsla *(top left and right)* • Full Skirt, self-drafted

Photo by Vatsla Watkins

Emily *(right)* • Full Skirt, self-drafted

Photo by Emily Hallman

Fit and Flare Dresses

(page 63)

Sarah [top and right] • Fit and Flare Dress, Vogue 8997

Photos by William Gunn

Emily [next page] • Fit and Flare Dress, self-drafted

Photo by Emily Hallman

Button-Up Shirt

(page 26)

Andrea *[right]* • Button-Up Shirt, Vogue 2691

Photo by Andrea Birkan

French Jacket

(page 153)

Andrea *[left]* • French Jacket, Vogue 7975, Custom Sheath Dress Pattern

Photo by Andrea Birkan

Karen *[far left]* • French Jacket, Susan Khalje The Classic French Jacket

Photo by Thomas B. Helm

French Jacket

(page 153)

Halter Dress or Top
(page 73)

Julie [top] • French Jacket, Susan Khalje Couture Classic French Jacket

Photo by William Gunn

Julie [left] • Halter Top, Kwik Sew 3308

Photo by William Gunn

Wrap
(page 161)

Sheath Dress
(page 56)

Sarah [top] • Wrap, McCall's 3880

Photo by William Gunn

Dorcas • Sheath Dress, Vogue American Designer Vera Wang 1585

Photo by Dorcas Ross

Bateau Top
(page 37)

Full Skirt
(page 21)

Julie • Bateau Top,
Closet Case Nettie Bodysuit;
Full Skirt, Just Patterns
Stephanie Skirt

Photo by Chris Smith

Pants

Jeans

Embodying the myths and ideals of American culture, jeans are one of the most worn garments on earth! Each decade embraced jeans in its own way, but throughout modern society, jeans are a considered a great equalizer—an enduring classic and *the* staple wardrobe item. You can rock a pair of great-fitting jeans at any age!

"Blue jeans are the most beautiful things since the gondola." DIANA VREELAND

History

Who could have predicted that jeans would become the uniform of choice for fashion editors, models, and corporate CEOs? The transition of the utilitarian workers' garb-goes-cool took the world by storm when ingenious fashion designers turned the cowboy pants into one of the most important fashion garments of the twentieth century.

After patenting the riveting process in 1873, Levi Strauss and his partner Jacob Davis became the originators of what is perhaps the most iconic garment in Western history. Contrary to popular belief, Levi Strauss & Co. did not invent what we know as "jeans"—there were plenty of denim pants made earlier. However, by adding rivets to stress points (such as the pockets and outer hip), Strauss and Davis found a way to make reinforced pants that stood the test of time. Today, original vintage jeans are highly prized by denim hunters and a single California Gold Rush–era pair can fetch five figures from serious collectors. Carpe *denim*!

Jeans from the 1950s represented teenage rebellion and rock and roll. Hollywood costume designers put all the bad boys in denim! The 60's counterculture used them as statements of creative expression—groovy hippies embellished their low-slung bell bottoms with embroidery, patches, and peace symbols. Major fashion designers were jumping on-board the jeans craze in the 70s and 80s, including Gloria Vanderbilt, Guess, Ralph Lauren, Sergio Valentino, Gucci, and Tommy Hilfiger. Brooke Shields's famous 1981 Calvin Klein ad was banned for being too provocative when she scandalously proclaimed, "Nothing comes between me and my Calvins!" And today, when Oprah Winfrey endorses her favorite brands, they fly off the shelves!

Characteristics

Whatever your preference for fit, there's a jeans pattern drafted to meet your desires. Today's straight leg, flared, boyfriend, and cropped styles tend to be cut slimmer through the hips and thighs, unlike baggier versions worn in previous decades. The skinny jean is one of the most popular women's denim styles due to its versatility to be dressed up or down. Dark wash or black slim jeans are practically today's dress pant. Every woman needs a pair of jeans in her hand-sewn, classic wardrobe!

Classic jeans construction details include:

* Two back pockets with custom stitched design

* Rivets

* Belt loops

* Front hip pockets, coin pocket optional

* Back yoke

* Contrasting topstitching

Sewing Tips

- One of our favorite features on recent jeans patterns is front pockets that extend into the front fly for subtle tummy control.

- Once thought to be an intimidating sewing project, the last several years have brought a proliferation of well drafted and easy to follow jeans patterns, tutorials, and sew-alongs. (See Resources: Related Articles, Videos, and Online Classes, page 174.) It's fun to perfect the fit and enjoy the satisfaction that comes with having created your own customized pair!

- We prewash and dry denim at least two times before beginning a project. Few things are more disheartening than putting in the time and effort to get the details just right and having your newly sewn jeans shrink in the first washing!

- Choose your sharpest scissors or a new rotary blade when cutting denim.

- Specific sewing machine needles for denim fabric (jeans needles) have reinforced blades to reduce the possibility of breakage and skipped stitches.

- Look for topstitching thread or try two strands of regular thread through a single needle as a substitute. Thread color can coordinate or contrast, depending on one's topstitching preference and skill level.

- An edgestitch presser foot can help ensure evenly spaced double topstitch rows.

- For professional-looking hems on knit fabrics, twin needles are an easy and helpful accessory for nearly any sewing machine. A twin needle sews two parallel rows of stitching on the right side and a row of zigzag stitches on the underside. This allows seams to stretch and prevents thread breakage.

- Stitch slowly and don't hesitate to stop and use the handwheel if your machine begins to protest!

- Experiment with tension and stitch length on fabric scraps before you start stitching on the actual garment fabric; a longer stitch length (3–4.5) may be necessary.

- A "hump-jumper" or a few taps of the hammer can be helpful to overcome fabric bulk when crossing over seam allowances.

- To prevent fabric shifting, try lessening presser foot pressure or basting seams. A walking foot can also come in handy. Strips of tissue paper that can be torn away after stitching help heavy denim glide through your machine more easily.

- Be sure to trim, grade, and overcast (or zigzag) each seam as it is sewn and press as you go, using a clapper if you have one.

Fabric Suggestions

Fortunately, denim is now sold in many weights, washes, colors, patterns, and prints. Serge denim, the traditional fabric used for making most jeans, is woven with 100% cotton fibers in a diagonal (or twill) pattern, which is sturdy and resilient. Though initially stiff, serge denim will fade and soften over time with repeated wear and laundering.

Considered by many to be the best quality, *selvedge denim* (with its durable "self-edge") is produced on traditional shuttle looms with 100% cotton thread and natural indigo dye. It has a distinctive clean finished edge with narrow red and white piping which is typically used for the outer leg seam. During the 1950s, many American manufacturers switched to projectile looms, which could weave up to ten times faster and lower production costs. Selvedge denim is worth the search and is available from online retailers.

The introduction of stretch fibers to denim fabrics eliminated any reason to suffer through an uncomfortable pair of jeans! *Do* invest in quality stretch denim to avoid sewing jeans that become baggy as the day wears on. A small amount of polyester in the fabric blend aids in fabric recovery. Stretch versions of cotton sateen, twill, and corduroy are all available in the ideal fabric weight for making jeans and are available in colorful, fun prints.

When it comes to jeans, white denim deserves its own category and will add freshness to any outfit! White jeans are the ultimate basic. Switch out bright white for seasonally appropriate winter white and you'll be good to go all year long!

Design Variations

Pull-on jeans patterns have recently hit the market, and we are believers! With all the bells and whistles of classic jeans and the comfort of a wide elastic waistband, you can enjoy authentic jeans styling details and no one will ever know!

How to Style

* Jeans with a blazer is an easy-to-wear fashion combination that provides a snappy pulled together look.

* Add one special accessory to draw attention to your style, such as a bright pair of shoes to the monochromatic look of a light chambray shirt and dark wash jeans.

* To successfully add jeans to your work wardrobe, stick to an otherwise neutral color palette (white shirt and black jacket or long cardigan). Accessorize with a necklace, great handbag and high heel pumps.

* High-waisted, wide leg jeans are a feminine, versatile, and flattering cut on many figures.

* For effortless Parisian chic, team a slightly cropped pair with a Breton striped shirt and backless loafer slides.

* White jeans are our bottoms of choice with a summer tunic!

* Jeans and T-shirts—weekends wouldn't be the same without them! Pick your favorite pair of jeans (consider the wash and fit) and wear them with your sneakers. Tuck in your T-shirt to accentuate high-waisted styles and keep the silhouette streamlined.

Who Wore It

ROSIE THE RIVETER • BING CROSBY, in a denim tuxedo in 1951
MARLON BRANDO in *The Wild One* • MARILYN MONROE in *River of No Return*
ELVIS PRESLEY • BROOKE SHIELDS (of course!) • BRUCE SPRINGSTEEN on the
album cover of *Born in the U.S.A.* • BARACK OBAMA, throwing out the first pitch
at the 2009 MLB All-Star Game • STEVE JOBS, with a black turtleneck
BRITNEY SPEARS • THE LEAD ACTRESSES in *Charlie's Angels* • KATE MOSS

Tailored Trousers: Fitted, Straight, Wide-Leg, Flared

Broadcasting the message that women can be powerful *and* sexy in trousers, Yves Saint Laurent was the first high-profile designer to promote tailored trousers for high-fashion wear with his revolutionary 1966 "Le Smoking" tuxedo suit. Encapsulating an attitude rather than the details of the garment, he proclaimed, "Fashions come and go, but style is forever." Professional, comfortable, and practical, a good pair of trousers is a foundation essential that anchors every classic wardrobe.

"I like being a woman, even in a man's world. After all, men can't wear dresses, but we can wear the pants." WHITNEY HOUSTON

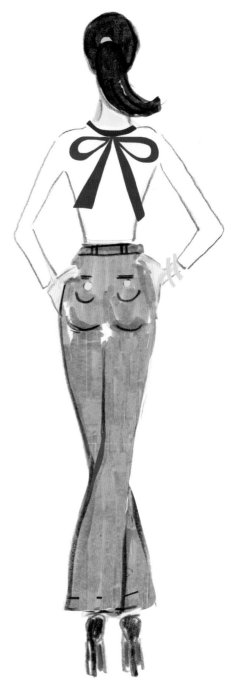

History

Who wears the pants? Considered an early symbol of equality for women, the first public appearances of women in pants began in the mid-1800s in the Western world. Women traded the tight corsets and heavy petticoats they had been wearing under their long skirts for wide, loose-fitting Turkish pants worn under knee-length skirts. The pants were named *bloomers* after the social activist and fashion reformer, Amelia Bloom. Although trousers as women's fashion didn't come into vogue until the twentieth century, women began wearing altered men's trousers for outdoor chores nearly a hundred years earlier.

By the 1930s, wide-leg trousers were becoming more commonplace in fashion magazine pages as well as on Hollywood A-listers, including Marlene Dietrich and Katharine Hepburn, who were seen wearing them on- and off-screen. In 1939, Vogue magazine featured its first spread to show women wearing trousers. Actresses and socialites wore the new pants to be just a little naughty and modern.

The post-war era led to the gradual erosion of prohibitions against wearing trousers in the workplace and schools and in 1972, girls across the United States cheered a change of school dress codes with the passage of Title IX, the nondiscrimination amendment declaring that wearing dresses could no longer be required.

Characteristics

Classic fly-front tailored trousers fall into several basic silhouettes.

FITTED (SLIM-CUT OR SKINNY) AND STRAIGHT TROUSERS

Slim-cut, skinny, or straight; heel-length, ankle-length, or slightly cropped—fitted trousers are the backbone of the smart casual dress code.

Slim-cut or skinny fitted trousers put a polished and streamlined spin on typical jeans styling.

Straight-leg trousers maintain the same width from knee to ankle. This style has a wider leg opening than fitted trousers. Classic straight-legged styles look good on nearly everyone because they are more forgiving for most body shapes.

Look for classic details such as slimming flat fronts and low-profile front pocket stays, fly fronts with zipper shield, rear welt pockets, and belt carriers. Curved waistbands allow for gap-free fitting opportunities for those with smaller waist to hip ratios.

WIDE-LEG AND FLARED TROUSERS

Wide-leg trousers maintain the same tailoring as their fitted counterparts. They are fitted at the waist through the top of the hips with a gradual widening which flows downward over the thighs for an easy draped effect.

Flared trousers usually taper inward slightly at the lower thigh and have a pronounced flare that starts just below the knee. Thanks to a wider hem that helps balance proportions, flared styles are more flattering than one might imagine.

Sewing Tips

- Quite possibly no other garment strikes as much fear in the heart of a sewist as trousers! Well-cut trousers can make you feel glamorous and confident and make your legs look long and slim! Experiment to find the type of trousers that creates the most flattering silhouette to complement the shape, proportion, and scale of your body. Try on a variety of ready-to-wear pants before deciding which style to sew.

- Proper fit, particularly along the tricky-to-fit crotch curve, is the key to trousers' comfort and attractive appearance. Trousers should fit comfortably at the waistline and fall smoothly over the hips and thighs with no pulling, gapping, or bunching; tailored, but not tight. For well-fitting trousers, the grainline must hang perpendicular to the floor.

- To achieve a trim, customized fit, taking accurate measurements, while wearing the same foundation garments you plan to wear with your trousers, is essential for success. There's no negotiating when sewing pants and trousers; you'll need to make at least one muslin for perfect fit (see The Importance of Sewing a Muslin, page 55), and a fit buddy is a bonus.

- Including details such as darts, angled front hip pockets, back welt pockets, pocket stays, and even stitched-down creases, helps to ensure that the trousers fit your body better than the best of ready-to-wear.

- A tip about what are commonly referred to as high-waisted pants: They're not "high-waisted" at all, but higher than what we've become accustomed to. Today's high-waisted pants hit at your natural waist, while appearing to lengthen your legs.

Fabric Suggestions

Your trouser style dictates fabric selection.

FITTED AND STRAIGHT TROUSERS

Figure-hugging slim and skinny trousers benefit from fabrics with some stretch fibers (elastane) to prevent their losing shape throughout the day. Look for new technical and performance blends that strike the perfect balance between structure and stretch. Jacquard texture adds a little luxury, especially when sewing with black fabrics.

Classically tailored trousers can be beautifully made in several light- to medium-weight fabrics, such as blends of linen, wool, cotton, silk, and in such fabrics as velvet, corduroy twill, ponte, gabardine, and suitings.

WIDE-LEG AND FLARED TROUSERS

Wide-leg trousers require medium-weight fabrics with sufficient drape; the wider the leg, the more the fabric should drape into soft folds. Some of our favorites include wool crepe, tencel, linen, rayon, and silk fibers in charmeuse, challis, chiffon, damask, and all types of woven and knit fabrics.

How to Style

• Slightly cropped and well tapered with classic pumps or ankle booties are always a winner. Combine with a simple tee or button-up shirt, posh jewelry, and a blazer for sophisticated polish.

• Breeze with ease through weekend errands! Casual khakis and cords deserve comfortable shoes for checking off chores, and any shoe will do! Experiment with flat booties, ballet flats, espadrilles, and your favorite sneakers.

• Evoke the allure of old-Hollywood glamour with a pair of wide-leg camel trousers, a silk animal print blouse, and a long rope of pearls.

• For a luxe cool weather evening outfit, deck yourself out in brocade evening trousers (straight or flared). Combine with a velvet turtleneck and a pair of embellished-toe flats for a party-perfect outfit.

Who Wore It

1947: KATHARINE HEPBURN in *Woman of the Year*

1969: BARBRA STREISAND, the first woman to attend the Oscars in trousers

1972: PAT NIXON, the first American First Lady to wear trousers in a national magazine

1974: 10-year-old TATUM O'NEAL, the youngest-ever recipient of an Academy Award for *Paper Moon*, wore a tuxedo to the ceremony

1977: DIANE KEATON in *Annie Hall*

1993: Representatives BARBARA MIKULSKI and CAROL MOSLEY BRAUN, on the Senate floor for the first time

2004: HILLARY CLINTON, the first First Lady to wear trousers in an official White House First Lady portrait

Palazzo Pants

What originated as beach pajamas gradually evolved into classic entertaining attire! From cocktail parties to island vacations, breezy palazzo pants make a bold statement no matter the fabric! Whether you sway with the music or gentle ocean breezes, try a pair of these easy-to-sew classics.

"When you don't dress like everybody else, you don't have to think like everybody else." IRIS APFEL

History

As pants began to enter the fashion scene, the palazzo pant appeared as resortwear. Palazzo pants, also known as pajama pants, dominated the beaches during the 1930s. Daywear palazzos, generally made from navy or white fabric, recall nautical themes, but beachwear featured soft pastel colors and big geometric prints. Eventually these dramatic pants became the ultimate hostess attire.

Characteristics

Typically cut to flare from an elastic waist, palazzo pants are extremely wide throughout the leg. The generous cut can make them look like a loose-fitting maxi skirt. Remember, the hem *must* skim the floor! Think long and loose. They're the most perfect, versatile piece imaginable to pack for a vacation. Plane rides, sightseeing, and dancing the night away represent just a fraction of this garment's travel and vacation friendly possibilities.

Sewing Tips

• Palazzo pants are one of the quickest and most satisfying styles you can create for "sew it today—wear it tonight" dressing. Using a simple casing for elastic, you can easily complete a pair in an hour or two.

• Ribbon can be attached to each end of the elastic and threaded through a buttonhole at the center front for a bow with a pretty, feminine finish.

• Add a little drama or a summer boho vibe, by creating visual interest using border prints for your palazzo pants!

• Styles featuring a waistband and belt loops look sophisticated and elegant with a self-fabric sash knotted at the waist or a narrow leather belt.

Fabric Suggestions

The voluminous silhouette of palazzo pants can handle sheer, fluid, and lightweight fabrics like jersey knits, georgette, silk, chiffon, voile, gauze, and batiks.

How to Style

For pleasing proportion, remember to wear a pared-down, simple top! We love palazzos topped with a tank or tee and a cropped denim jacket.

Who Wore It

KATHARINE HEPBURN

MARLENE DIETRICH

LUPITA NYONG'O

Capri Pants

Did you know revealing the ankle bone is thought to be sexy? In 1948, the Capri pant was considered a revolutionary design after years of women wearing masculine and tailored pants. By the mid-1950s, practically every European designer included Capris in their collections, introducing the concept of "casual chic." Typically sewn from stretch fabrics, these comfortable pants are major players in smart capsule wardrobes.

"Despite the forecast, live like it's Spring!" LILLY PULITZER

History

This style of pants could very well be a tribute to Mary Tyler Moore who caused a fashion sensation on *The Dick Van Dyke Show* in the early 1960s. The slim black Capris frequently worn by her character, Laura Petrie, have been referred to as the most important costume on TV! Women rarely wore pants in public and certainly not Capris! Due to the sponsors' fears that the tight fit was too suggestive for society norms, show producers allowed Moore to wear the pants in only one scene per episode.

German fashion designer Sonja de Lennart introduced Capri pants to the fashion scene as part of her 1948 Capri Collection which was inspired by her love of the island, Capri. The collection also included a wide swinging skirt, high-neck blouse, a belt, and a hat. Costume designer Edith Head admired Lennart's innovate fashion aesthetic and had the entire Capri Collection sewn for Audrey Hepburn in the 1952 movie *Roman Holiday*. Two years later, Hepburn also wore the Capri pants in *Sabrina*, and soon the pants were the rage and popularized by high-profile actresses and celebrities.

Sixty years later, Capris have found their way into mainstream dressing, and every women's clothing store offers a seasonal collection of Capri and cropped pants with compatible styling options.

Characteristics

The Capri pant is defined as a fitted ¾-length pant ending between the knee and the ankle with an outer side slit for comfort. Designer Sonja de Lennart first offered Capri pants in two different lengths: the shorter length for summer and a longer length for winter. The fitted pant was designed to emphasize a shapely feminine leg. The closure features a side or back zipper. While the terms "Capri pants" and "cropped pants" are used interchangeably today, we're sticking with the original and classic term!

Sewing Tips

• We recommend making a muslin in an inexpensive stretch cotton for accurate fitting (see The Importance of Sewing a Muslin, page 55). Capris can be sewn very quickly in the fashion fabric once the fitting is perfected in the muslin stage.

• Since Capris are designed to emphasize the shape of the leg you must decide on the length before cutting out your fashion fabric. Altering the length might result in the need to gently reshape the pattern piece, which should be done before cutting the fashion fabric.

• Look for patterns with a shaped waistline, which is more flattering, doesn't gape, and keeps tops tucked in place. For a contemporary technique, attach the back waistband pieces to the back pants pieces and insert an invisible zipper starting at the top of the waistband. You'll avoid the necessity of a hook and eye, and the zipper will disappear as it is designed to do.

• If your pants do not have a waistband, try using Petersham ribbon as the facing. The braided edge of Petersham allows you to shape the ribbon with steam and is our preferred facing for skirts and pants (see Resources: Trims, Tools, and Notions, page 174).

Fabric Suggestions

Turn this simple silhouette into your own signature look! Capris and cropped pants work best in stretch woven fabrics. Try bright feminine colors, bold prints, and graphic designs, similar to those designs used by the 1950 designers. Small vintage prints, windowpane checks, gingham, tropical florals, or Pucci-style abstracts are perfectly charming for this style pant. Use stretch cottons, twills, poplins, sateens, and lightweight denims blended with Lycra, elastane, or spandex for premium comfort and fit. Keep the ratio approximately 97% cotton to 3% stretch fiber, because too much stretch can result in baggy knees. Stretch gabardine is a good choice for a dressier pant.

How to Style

- Capri pants adapt to most any look you're seeking, but bear in mind successful styling is all about proportions. Don't look frumpy!

- The Capri pant creates horizontal lines, which can make you look shorter and wider. For a long and lean silhouette, keep your pants slim and forgo the details such as patch pockets and cuffs.

- Capri pants certainly showcase your shoes so let those leopard print pumps be the star of the show! They're perfect with a pair of black cropped pants.

- For the Lilly Pulitzer look, sew your cropped pants in a tropical floral print. Pair with gold sandals and a simple bright top.

- Cropped pants are often labeled *tunic pants* since they provide the perfect balance for the flowy top. It's a great combination! Try wearing a thigh length tunic and simple shoes with your pants.

- Simple chic is easy to attain with this slim pant! Monochromatic ensembles, capped off with a contrasting sweater or jacket (shorter than knee length) and pumps will take you most anywhere!

- Wear them with a jeans jacket, T-shirt, and your favorite fashion sneakers for classic weekend dressing!

- Channel your inner starlet by pairing your Capris with a fitted sweater, halter top, or cropped button-up tied at the waist.

- A sweater set, cute ballet flats, and Capris are a classic look, attractive and practical!

Shoes

You can transform the look of your Capris with a simple change of shoes.

• Heels of most heights work well, but choose streamlined shoes over chunky ones that will throw your look out of proportion.

• Pumps in general elongate the leg and put a polished spin on these simple pants.

• Higher booties also provide an elongated look—the top of the boot should just clear the hemline.

• You'll be as classic as Audrey Hepburn when pairing your cropped pants with ballet flats.

• Choose fashion sneakers over bulky athletic shoes!

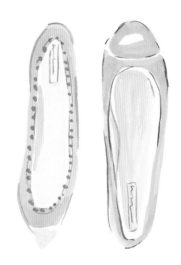

Who Wore It

Brigitte wore hers with slippers, Ava wore hers with heels, and Marilyn … she wore hers with sneakers. They knew a classic when they saw one and they knew how to make it their own!

BRIGITTE BARDOT • DORIS DAY • JANE RUSSELL • KATHARINE HEPBURN • GINA LOLLOBRIGIDA • AVA GARDNER ELIZABETH TAYLOR • JACQUELINE KENNEDY • MARILYN MONROE • KIM NOVAK • SOPHIA LOREN • ANITA EKBERG MARY TYLER MOORE • ALL THE ACTRESSES in *Grease* • AUDREY HEPBURN

Outerwear

Jeans-Style Jacket

The cowboy era faded, but the jeans jacket became part of American fashion history, first signifying the rebellion of the 50s and eventually becoming ingrained in our collective fashion culture. Every hip ready-to-wear label now offers its own version. Jeans get all the glory but the jeans-style jacket, despite its modest origins, is quite essential in a stylish wardrobe!

"Denim is a love that never fades."

ELIO FIORUCCI

History

Although indigo dye was crucial to garment production along the trade route known as the Silk Road more than 200 years ago, late nineteenth-century France is credited with naming denim after workers in the city of Nîmes ("*de Nîmes*" became *denim*!). The workers wore dark blue coats to differentiate them from higher level bosses who wore white or gray. The Levi Strauss & Co. created its first versions of denim jeans and jackets as durable utility garments during the California Gold Rush, around 1880.

Characteristics

The original and classic fit and style of the denim jacket tends to stay consistent (except the over-size 80's acid-wash styles), so that a great denim jacket lasts for decades and only improves with age! Jackets from the 60s, 70s, and 90s all have a similar cut and fit, and are typically made of 100% quality cotton, unlike some of today's polyester stretch blends. A snug, shirtlike fit through the shoulders and a length that hits at the high hip is most universally flattering, while a more relaxed fit allows for layering over your favorite tees, shirts, turtlenecks, and sweaters.

Sewing Tips

- Sewing a jeans jacket doesn't differ much from sewing a shirt, it just needs the addition of some fun hardware à la rivets, snaps, and jean-style buttons!

- Your topstitching skills need to shine here, so lots of sample stitching and practice is essential.

- An edgestitch foot can be your best friend for the seemingly miles of decorative stitching that can be used to personalize your denim jacket.

- Use size 80/12 or 90/14 needles to accommodate thicker topstitching thread and the weight of the fabric.

- Specialty topstitching thread is available, or you can stitch with two strands of regular thread for greater visual impact. Be sure to use regular thread that matches your jacket in the bobbin.

- The weight of the interfacing you choose should be compatible with the fiber content and weight of your fabric.

- A hammer or "hump jumper" is invaluable to flatten bulky seam intersections and provides easier sewing over multiple fabric layers.

- Flat-fell seams are used on ready-to-wear denim jackets, but mock flat-fell seams constructed with edge-finished seams, pressed to one side, and topstitched are a perfectly acceptable substitution and time saving option. (See Resources: Sewing Instruction and Alteration Books, page 175.)

Fabric Suggestions

With the proliferation of quality denim available to the home sewing market, you'll have a nearly unlimited selection of fabrics from which to choose. Classic blue indigo denim in any wash or weight that suits your style and climate is the traditional route.

Stretch denim or twill in cotton or blends is ideal for comfortable, lighter-weight jackets and can be found in every color of the rainbow including geometric prints and florals.

For those who like to think outside the box, consider making your jeans-style jacket in leather, suede, cotton twill, corduroy, or velveteen!

How to Style

• Mix washes (colors) when wearing your jacket with your favorite jeans to avoid a monochromatic look.

• For an unexpectedly feminine look, wear a jeans jacket over a floaty lace or floral skirt. The slim upper proportions help balance the volume of the skirt.

• Try your favorite denim jacket under a winter coat to add a layer of warmth.

• Top a jeans jacket with an oversized scarf or shawl for a fabulous fall combination.

• Hand or machine embroidery and appliqué on denim are trending in a big way again, and there's no better way to create your own personal style statement than to add this embellishment to your own denim wardrobe.

• For a city-chic vibe, try wearing over a dark turtleneck with an animal print skirt and tall boots.

• Consider a white denim jacket for a crisp, clean summer topper that pairs perfectly with airy maxi skirts and shorts.

• For a failsafe style upgrade, flip up your cuffs, pop your collar, and strut your denim!

Who Wore It

LEVI STRAUSS

THE MARLBORO MAN

JAMES DEAN

MARILYN MONROE

ROBERT REDFORD

BRUCE SPRINGSTEEN

SUSAN SARANDON and

GEENA DAVIS in *Thelma and Louise*

MADONNA

Blazer

While Brooks Brothers popularized the blazer for men, Ralph Lauren showed women how to wear this classic garment. The tailored, single-breasted blazer creates flattering angles from the shoulders down. Well-cut blazers in luxury fabrics only get better with age! Along with the white shirt, many stylists recommend the tailored blazer as the number one must-have garment.

"I'm interested in longevity, timelessness, style—not fashion."

RALPH LAUREN

History

One button or two, rolled collar or notched? There are many design versions of the basic single-breasted blazer.

In 1825, the blazer was created as a "uniform" for the sport of rowing. The Lady Margaret Boat Club, the rowing club of St. John's College in Cambridge, wore *blazing* red jackets, which became known as *blazers* due to the color. Other rowing teams adopted the style and wore blazers in their own school colors. Not only did the blazers keep the rowers warm, but they helped the spectators identify the teams from ashore. Rowers began wearing their blazers on campus as a status symbol. Soon many sports teams wore blazers and the term blazer started to refer to any sporting jacket cut from a lightweight fabric. The blazer eventually became an established wardrobe item among Europeans and the style evolved. Brooks Brothers is credited for popularizing the blazer in the United States.

On the womenswear scene, as the popularity of the bustle declined, women's tailoring grew. European women began wearing tailored jackets in the nineteenth century for outdoor activities, but as American women entered the workforce, their clothes became more streamlined. Tailored suits, originally a jacket and long skirt, became the norm for the working woman. As women adopted menswear styles, the blazer worked its way into most women's wardrobes regardless of their professional status.

Characteristics

An outer layer garment, the blazer is a minimally designed, collared garment with long sleeves, and front button closures. Fitted from the shoulders with shoulder pads, blazers emphasize the shape of the body but are not overly fitted to better accommodate garments worn underneath such as shirts, sweaters, and T-shirts.

Most women's blazers are sewn from high-quality and durable fabrics and feature a few standard characteristics:

• Either a notched lapel and collar or a rolled shawl collar

• A traditional length, falling between the mid- and lower-crotch

• Two-piece sleeves, which are vented and hemmed slightly shorter than the shirt sleeve

• A back vent for easy movement

• Either welts or patch front pockets, with or without a flap

Warm-weather blazers are often left unlined and finished with Hong Kong seams. Cool weather blazers, on the other hand, are lined with fabrics ranging from synthetic materials such as polyester and rayon to natural materials including cotton and silk. Lined blazers generally hold their structure better than unlined ones and are more durable and significantly warmer.

Sewing Tips

- Sewing a blazer is not for the sewist seeking immediate gratification, but is achievable by those with fundamental skills. Select an easy style, as indicated on the pattern envelope, for your first blazer. Not only will you get a better grasp of the sewing process, you'll gain an understanding of your ideal fit and personal style aesthetic.

- Books and classes (online and in-person) are readily available for those seeking to develop tailoring skills. (See Resources: Related Articles, Videos, and Online Classes, page 174, and Sewing Instruction and Alteration Books, page 175.)

Fabric Suggestions

We stop just short of saying any fabric goes! Durable fabrics make the best blazers and there are many, including: worsted wool, stretch wool, wool crepe, flannel, velvet, linen, tweed, jacquard weaves, sateen, seersucker, corduroy, leather, and even stable knits.

Herringbones, houndstooth plaids, glen plaids, florals, pinstripes, windowpane checks, and embroidered fabrics are but a few textile patterns you can use to bring new dimension to your blazer.

Design Variations

Blazers take on their own unique personality with variations in a few basic details. Fabric color and pattern create different types of blazers, from those suitable for evening attire, officewear, to rowing competitions and other sporting events. Button choice also sets the tone of the blazer: Brass buttons reinforce its traditional design, while leather buttons (and elbow patches) put an academic spin on the blazer. A monogrammed breast pocket conveys a preppy spirit, and bright colors create chic statement pieces.

To put a modern touch on this classic silhouette, consider using a fresh print lining or contrasting fabric for the undercollar.

How to Style

Making a blazer work for you is an easy task. This ubiquitous classic can go the distance with several of the clothes you have in your closet!

The navy blazer adds sleek structure to your workweek style. Consider the following possibilities:

• With a pencil skirt or slim pants and a pair pumps

• Over a chambray shirt and white T-shirt with white jeans

• Worn with a blue-and-white–stripe bateau neckline top, and yellow skinny jeans; for a more nautical look, switch the yellow jeans for white wide-leg trousers

• With dresses, skirts, pants, casual khakis, and leggings for a quick, put-together look

• With a sheath of matching or contrasting colors

• Bright-colored jeans, white T-shirts, and silk scarves for streetwear chic

• With a gingham shirt and espadrilles

• With printed ankle pants and flats

For alternatives to the classic navy blazer, try sewing:

• Seersucker blazer and matching Capris paired with espadrilles for summer chic

• Long floral sateen blazer to wear with jeans and boots for boho flair

• Printed velvet blazer styled with cami and slim ankle pants for the theater

• Tweed blazer with fringed edges to soften the look of the menswear style. Pair it with leather pants.

• White blazer for cool confidence in hot weather

• Ponte knit blazer for traveling in style

Who Wore It

Many women have followed in the footsteps of Katharine Hepburn to make this menswear garment not only acceptable, but stylish, feminine, and classic. Kate Middleton rocks the navy blazer on a regular basis in traditional splendor along with countless high-profile celebrities who have adopted the blazer to fit their style. They include:

HILLARY CLINTON • MADONNA
DIANE KEATON • BEYONCÉ
LAUREN HUTTON • EVA LONGORIA
JENNIFER LOPEZ • RIHANNA

Trench Coat

Gravitas, dignity, bravery, mystery ... and that's just the beginning. Designed for powerful men, worn by leading actors and femme fatales, the trench coat's longevity surpasses its powerhouse image thanks to its marriage of function and style. You need one!

"Everyone in the world should have a trench coat, and there should be a trench coat for everyone in the world. It does not matter your age; it doesn't matter your gender."

ANGELA AHRENDTS

History

The 150-year battle continues: Which luxury clothing manufacturer invented the trench coat—Aquascutum or Burberry? Each patented a waterproof fabric.

In the 1850s, John Emary patented a fabric for his company, Aquascutum, to replace the non-breathable rubberized cotton of men and women's outerwear. Several years later, in 1879, Thomas Burberry invented gabardine and submitted a design for an army officer's raincoat to the United Kingdom War Office in 1901. No matter who invented the trench coat, Burberry took the style, ran with it, and turned the military garment into an iconic classic.

As a military garment, the back vent eliminated odors and kept the coat breathable, the large pockets held gear, shoulder tabs provided a way to attach items such as epaulettes and rank insignia, the detachable lining was used as a blanket, the collar buttons at the neck were designed to secure gas masks, cuff straps were used to secure binoculars, and the length of the coat was designed to be short enough to clear the mud of the trenches.

The military officers loved their trench coats and continued to wear them after the war. Burberry and Aquascutum began manufacturing trench coats as sportswear and soon the trench coat began to appear on the silver screen. Humphrey Bogart catapulted the trench coat to celebrity status through his performances in *The Maltese Falcon*, *Casablanca*, and *The Big Sleep*. Soon the trench coat was adopted by fashion forward females. It quickly rose to prominence thanks (in part) to the dramatic black-and-white photographs of high-profile celebrities such as Marlene Dietrich, Brigitte Bardot, Audrey Hepburn, and Catherine Deneuve.

Characteristics

The specific design features of the original military garment have changed very little, a classic trench coat includes the following:

* Usually made of waterproof cotton gabardine

* Removable wool lining

* Typically made in shades of khaki or beige

* Double-breasted front closing with 10 buttons

* Storm flap, the double layer around the shoulders which keeps wind-driven rain out

* Wide lapels

* Pockets that button closed

* Raglan sleeves

* Waist belt with belt carriers sewn to the coat body

* Buckled straps around the cuffs

* Shoulder tabs

* Length ranging from just above the ankle to just above the knee

Variations of this classic mainstay include a sleeveless or sheath-style dress or shirt made up in lightweight fabric. Many field jackets feature trench coats details. Originally designed for hunting, Barbour-style jackets have also transitioned from functional to fashionable!

Sewing Tips

- The trench coat is not a project for beginners, but it is very doable for intermediate sewists.

- Gather all your notions and hardware ahead of time. You want to ensure the finishes of the grommets, buckles, and buttons are coordinated.

- When fitting the coat, take into consideration what you plan to wear underneath. We recommend making a toile (see The Importance of Sewing a Muslin, page 55) from an inexpensive midweight fabric rather than lightweight muslin.

- Practice your bound buttonholes, or engage a tailor to sew your buttonholes. It's okay and doesn't mean you are cheating!

- As with the denim jacket, topstitching details are crucial for this garment. Practice topstitching with a heavier thread on scrap fabric before stitching your fashion fabric. Another option is to pull two threads through a single needle, but again practice on scrap fabric to make sure your topstitching is acceptable.

Fabric Suggestions

The classic trench coat is sewn in a neutral color of midweight gabardine or twill fabric.

More than 100 years after its debut, the coat's original design remains intact, but variations continue to surface. Fabric variations for warm weather may include waxed cotton, poplin, and stretch cotton, and you need not be limited to neutral solid colors. However, regardless of the climate, florals, plaids, animal prints, and bright colors bring a pop of fun to the classic styling.

How to Style

This garment's styling options might surprise you!

- Knot the belt for waistline definition.

- Try the Meghan Markle look by wearing a sleeveless pastel trench dress with neutral pumps.

- Consider sewing a "trench blouse." A white trench blouse offers both professional and sporty dressing. Pair it with tailored trousers for the office and khaki skinny pants for a casual afternoon.

- While the traditional neutral colors work well with a spectrum of garments, a bright color, knee-length trench coat is feminine, casual, and perfect with jeans and sneakers.

- Take the *Garden & Gun* approach by sewing a Barbour-style field jacket paired with jeans and flat boots.

Who Wore It

HUMPHREY BOGART • AUDREY HEPBURN • BRIGITTE BARDOT • DICK TRACY • INGRID BERGMAN

SHERLOCK HOLMES • MEGHAN MARKLE • MARLENE DIETRICH • JACQUELINE KENNEDY • OPRAH WINFREY

French Jacket

The French jacket is a world-renowned symbol of status and class. It is effortlessly chic, always appropriate, and lasts forever. Originally designed by Coco Chanel, this class act looks as fabulous with your favorite jeans as it does with a matching skirt for more formal occasions.

"The best things in life are free; the second best are very expensive."

COCO CHANEL

History

Darling ... now you can have your cake and eat it too!

The French jacket was revolutionary in that, for the first-time menswear was interpreted in feminine form with movement less restricted than in fashions previously available to women. The style was first conceived by Gabrielle (Coco) Chanel when she borrowed sportswear from her beau, the Duke of Westminster, and began experimenting with incorporating fibers like silk and cotton into traditional Scottish tweeds. She felt the most important part of her design work was to ensure that women could move with ease in her designs. The French jacket was the perfect choice for post-war women who were trying to build a career in the male-dominated workplace. In 1954, at the age of 71, Coco began offering the jacket in pastel colors at her Paris atelier. These jackets quickly became an international sensation. They were highly sought after by upwardly mobile Americans after Jackie Kennedy frequently appeared in the now infamous pink Chanel-style suit. Thought to be a designer original, the pink suit was an authorized copy made by Chez Ninon in New York.

Characteristics

Many have long admired this garment for its timeless elegance on the outside, never understanding that the magic on the inside is the real story.

The French jacket is constructed by quilting lofty bouclé to silk lining with rows of stitches that are all but invisible from the outside, but produce a sumptuous double layer that hugs the body almost like a sweater and feels like heaven to wear. Historically, the jacket has been short and boxy; however, modern versions often display a silhouette more fitted through the torso, in lengths from high hip to your favorite coat length!

Additional features include a high, small armscye; three-piece sleeves; ornate braid trims on outer edges (including sleeve vents); showy buttons; and the iconic hem chain, which was originally intended to counter-balance weighty decorative elements and prevent the jacket from slipping forward on the shoulders. Now the iconic hem chain is symbolic of couture elegance!

Sewing Tips

- The creation of a French jacket is time-consuming, with many sewing construction steps which may seem daunting. The steps are really just a process and are within reach of any sewist with intermediate level skills and the desire to own this most coveted of clothing items. Once the construction of the garment is presented in manageable steps, it's quite doable for anyone with determination.

- The bonus of making this jacket yourself, of course, is that you save many thousands of dollars over the purchasing price tag, which begins at $5,000 for a Chanel ready-to-wear version and $40,000 for a haute couture original.

- The key to making this classic is to take your time. Enjoy this journey, and remember you are creating an heirloom-quality jacket using time-honored haute couture techniques. Luxuriate in the pleasure of working with the finest materials and the meditative state of mind that hand stitching can produce as you focus on forming one perfectly consistent stitch after another (see Resources: Sewing Instruction and Alteration Books, page 175).

- To begin, make a muslin or toile (see The Importance of Sewing a Muslin, page 55), work to refine the muslin for perfect fit, and then remove the stitching to so you can use the fabric pieces as the actual pattern pieces to cut the bouclé fabric (see Resources: Related Articles, Videos, and Online Classes, page 174, and Sewing Instruction and Alteration Books, page 175).

- The perfect trim can be difficult to source. While you can purchase gimps, braids, and vintage trims, you might consider making self-fringe; knitting or crocheting a trim with complementary fancy ribbon yarns; layering trims for added dimension; or incorporating sequins or beads for an evening-style French jacket. There's no limit to the types of suitable trims and the possibilities they offer to personalize your masterpiece.

- Prominent and jewelrylike statement buttons are typically placed on the jacket's pockets and sleeve vents. Buttons with hand-worked buttonholes may be used as front closures, but mastering these buttonholes requires much practice and 100 percent perfect execution. Jacket hooks recessed along the front edges and hidden between the boucle and silk lining are a completely acceptable alternative to buttonholes, as is a zipper.

Fabric Suggestions

For a project that is estimated by many to take as many as 70 to 100 hours to complete, you'll want to source the very best quality fabrics and trims your budget allows. Lofty, textural boucles are the most suitable fabric choice, to ensure the quilting stitches nestle into the fabric and become nearly imperceptible on the exterior.

Silk charmeuse is the lining of choice; its satiny smooth luster feels wonderful against your skin. Printed silk linings add a splash of fun on the inside and you might also want to consider purchasing extra fabric to make a matching silk blouse.

How to Style

There's a place in every woman's wardrobe for this classic, and you'll be proud to say you made it yourself. Far from being one dimensional and too precious to save for all but special occasions, a French jacket can be both ladylike *and* edgy. A few of our favorite ways to wear it are with …

… skinny jeans, a white shirt, and booties.

… cropped trousers, classic white button-up shirt, and ballet flats.

… wide-leg trousers and a turtleneck.

… a matching skirt, as a suit.

… over a sheath dress.

… a lace or leather skirt.

… a pashmina wrap.

Who Wore It

COCO CHANEL • BARBARA WALTERS PRINCESS DIANA • ANNA WINTOUR QUEEN ELIZABETH at London Fashion Week 2012 • JACQUELINE KENNEDY on November 22, 1963 • CATE BLANCHETT in *Blue Jasmine*

Last but Not Least

Menswear Pajamas

At the end of the day there's nothing like slipping into a pair of crisply pressed pajamas. Not only for sleeping and reading in bed, classic menswear pajamas are the ultimate loungewear for lazy weekend mornings with the newspaper or a rainy-day Netflix binge. Think of them as the adult alternative to sweats and tees. You spend a lot of time in pajamas, so why not sew some that make you feel as good as the rest of your wardrobe?

"One of the key moments in my life was the discovery that I could get away with wearing pajamas most of the time." HUGH HEFNER

History

You don't need to lounge around the Playboy Mansion to enjoy a good pair of pajamas! Originally, pajamas were loose lightweight drawstring pants worn throughout much of Asia, especially India. The origin of the word pajama dates to the Ottoman Empire and comes from the Hindi *paejama* or *paijama*, meaning "leg clothing." Before the 1800s, people generally wore their undergarments to bed rather than a separate garment designated for sleeping.

Madcap comedies of the 1930s and 40s sparked the craze for men's style pajamas when Claudette Colbert's character borrowed a pair from Clark Gable's character in *It Happened One Night* and Myrna Loy as Nora Charles wore them to lounge and sip martinis in *The Thin Man*.

With the popularity of unisex styling during the 1970s, pajamas were often menswear inspired. More recently, bedtime pajamas have begun to see daylight, an unlikely but enduring fashion trend.

Characteristics

Traditional menswear-style pajamas consist of a lightweight, button-front, jacketlike top, often featuring lapels and a chest pocket with a matching pair of drawstring or elastic-waisted bottoms, usually made of cotton, linen, silk, satin, or flannel. Pant and sleeve lengths can be short or long. The finished edges of better quality PJs are often outlined with piping.

Sewing Tips

- Premade piping is adequate and available in a fairly wide range of colors, but for a small investment of time and a $1/2$ yard of fabric, you can make your own custom bias tape in a matching or complimentary fabric. Turning bias tape and inexpensive cording into piping with a zipper foot or specialty piping foot takes very little time. (See Resources: Trims, Tools, and Notions, page 174.)

- To ensure neat and evenly applied piping, always sew the piping to the right side of one layer of fabric first. Then pin the corresponding fabric piece to the second layer with right sides together. Join the layers by stitching directly over the first row of stitching. This ensures a crisp, clean, and consistent outline of piping with no visible stitching lines on the right side of the garment.

- A monogrammed pocket brings a special touch of indulgence and is easy to do with today's home embroidery machines. What a welcome gift to create for a special recipient!

- For waistbands, insert soft, wide elastic in a self-fabric casing or insert a drawstring instead of elastic in the casing.

- Buttons and buttonholes are the customary front closing for the top, but if buttonholes are your bane, snaps are an easy-to-install alternative.

Fabric Suggestions

For day-in-day-out comfort and practicality, natural fiber fabrics such as cotton poplin, shirting, lawn, voile, gingham, and seersucker are always good choices. Liberty of London cotton lawn is the pajama fabric of our dreams! Quality designer "quilting" cottons in cheerful print coordinates make one-of-a-kind pajama sets, and tencel twill is a lovely economical alternative to four-ply silk. French terry is ideal for cooler weather and what would the holidays be without a new pair of plaid flannel PJs! Flannel backed satin, a great choice for warmth and coziness on the inside, belies its luxe exterior, while silk charmeuse is decadent for a lavish, "champagne for breakfast" pajama.

How to Style

All you need is a good pair of slippers, a classic robe, and a breakfast tray!

Who Wore It

MERYL STREEP and STANLEY TUCCI in *Julie & Julia*
DIANE KEATON and JACK NICHOLSON
in *Something's Gotta Give*
MEG RYAN in *You've Got Mail*
OPRAH WINFREY

Wraps

The divas of old Hollywood knew how to make an entrance—*strut, stop, and toss*! Who doesn't want to stop traffic? Looking to transform an outfit ... or your outlook? All you need is a wrap, just make sure you know what to do with it!

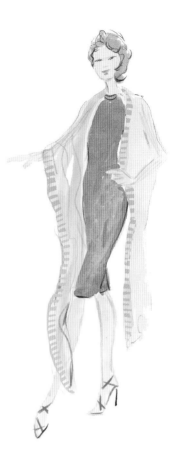

"The most attractive accessory a woman has is confidence." AUDREY HEPBURN

History

Whether you're looking for warmth or simply wishing to accessorize, wraps have you covered. From the mountains of India, to land of the gentry, the wrap's role in fashion history spans continents and centuries. Consider the history of the shawl, a popular version of a wrap. Upon receiving a gift of socks woven from Kashmiri goat hair, the King of Kashmir, Sultan Qutub-ud-Din, and his craftsman Ali Hamadani, started a shawl-weaving company in the fourteenth century, and from it, the famed Kashmir shawls were born.

Shawls, throughout history, tended to represent the textiles and artisans of indigenous cultures. Chinese shawls featured hand-painted silk, while Spanish shawls were embroidered. Egyptian shawls, made from assuit, a textile of cotton or linen mesh combined with small strips of metal, have been found in tombs dating prior to 1500 BC.

Fast forward to the 1920s, when beaded capelets and oversized shawls graced the shoulders of flappers and socialites who wanted to cover their shoulders but not their dress! Capelets often featured elaborately beaded art deco designs and were considered works of art. Silk and lightweight velvet evening shawls, embellished with hand-painted Asian and Egyptian motifs were trimmed in long strands of fringe, often reaching to the ankles.

Scenes from *The Great Gatsby* film and TV's *Downton Abbey* beautifully capture the decorative attire of this period. The great cultural shawls were constructed from very expensive fabrics eventually leading to variations in textiles, shapes and sizes for the less affluent.

During the early twentieth century, French designers such as Paul Poiret introduced the fur stole in their collections. These elegant wraps, thrown over the shoulders, were immediately embraced by socially prominent women. While the fur stole's popularity has never waned, toppers such as fur tippets and collars soon entered the fashion scene.

Today women swaddle, drape, cover, and accessorize with wraps of all shapes, sizes, and fabrics. What's a classic wrap, you ask? ... The choice is yours!

Characteristics

While classic wraps such as shawls, stoles, ruanas, scarves, and capelets possess unique characteristics, they are all accessorylike, sleeveless garments that loosely cover the upper body. A shawl is sewn from a single piece of fabric, while the classic stole can be sewn from three shaped pieces to better hug the shoulders. Shawls are rarely lined, but stoles are always lined.

Often sewn from luxury fabrics, think of the wrap as the icing on the cake!

Sewing Tips

* Sewing an evening wrap is an opportunity to have fun with unique and specialty fabrics since the construction process is simple.

* Many evening wrap patterns are available and feature dozens of variations.

* A rolled hem is an ideal edge finish for sheer fabric wraps. Practice stitching it on the sewing machine and by hand.

* When sewing with furs, keep the vacuum handy and be prepared for the fur to fly. The Bluprint blog (see Resources: Related Articles, Videos, and Online Classes, page 174) offers valuable tips to enhance your fur-sewing experience.

* Remember both sides of wraps are visible, so take your time for a professional result.

Fabric Suggestions

This is the garment for which to use that special novelty piece of fabric you stashed years ago! Fabrics need not be expensive, but the wrap is a statement piece and it will garner attention, so fabric choice is important. Formal fabrics such as silk taffeta, embroidered chiffon, silk organza, brocade, jacquard, velvet, sequins, silk shantung, silk dupioni, and tulle compliment black-tie and cocktail attire and are perfect choices for eveningwear wraps.

Now available in every conceivable color and print, faux furs provide an affordable and ethical solution for warmly wrapping up in style. Don't forget cashmere, and soft wool flannels for cold winter days. The terms *faux fur* and *fur* are used interchangeably in this chapter!

Metallic linens add shimmer to casual dressing, while feathers bring out your inner diva. African wax prints bring any outfit to life while a leather stole is downright edgy.

Consider mixing textiles. Chiffon and satin provide a lovely contrast, and work well as tie closures when combined with textiles such as velvet fur/faux fur and sequins, or try trimming wool flannel in bias leather strips.

Design Variations

Many wraps feature a pull-through closure much like a large buttonhole. Nonslippery fabrics are perfect for this detail. If you're seeking a more discreet method of closing, try concealed closures such as hidden snaps or hook and eyes.

How to Style

• Embellish any wrap with tassels, fringe, lace, beads, embroidery, and fabric paints. Or consider adding a ruffle for a feminine touch.

• A cleverly styled classic wrap keeps you warm and starts a conversation! Finding the right proportional balance is the key.

• Make a *ruana*, also known as the blanket wrap, in a soft plaid flannel and style it with skinny jeans and booties.

• Complement a wedding gown with a white fur stole.

• Go for dramatic style by draping a red taffeta ruffled wrap over a slim black silhouette.

• Complete a dupioni sheath ensemble with a two-toned reversible wrap: one side in matching dupioni and the other in a contrasting color.

• Pair your dreamy pastel cashmere wrap with white jeans or a favorite floral dress for winter warmth on a cool spring day.

Who Wore It

ROSALIND RUSSELL in *Auntie Mame* • ANN-MARGRET • MARILYN MONROE • ELIZABETH TAYLOR
CARMEN, lead character in Georges Bizet's *Carmen* • PRIYANKA CHOPRA • OPRAH WINFREY
MICHELLE DOCKERY in *Downton Abbey*

PROJECT
The Modern Classic
Pencil Skirt

The Modern Classic Pencil Skirt features a subtle bell-shaped silhouette, which accentuates a woman's curves and provides the feminine flair a pencil skirt deserves! With a dartless front and three-piece shaped waistband, our multisize pattern is available in sizes 2–22. Sew this garment in midweight fabrics for any occasion.

Materials

Fashion fabric—60″ (150 cm) wide:

All sizes: 1 yard (1 m)

Fashion fabric and lining—45″ (110 cm) wide:

Sizes 2–6: 1 yard (1 m) each

Sizes 8–10: 1¹⁄₈ yards (1.1 m) each

Sizes 12–16: 1³⁄₈ yards (1.3 m) each

Sizes 18–22: 1⁵⁄₈ yards (1.5 m) each

Fusible interfacing: ¹⁄₂ yard (45.7 cm)

Invisible zipper: 7″–9″ (17.8–22.9 cm)

(Shorter zipper for smaller sizes; longer zipper for 12+ sizes)

Matching thread

Hem tape (*optional*)

Invisible zipper presser foot

Fabric marking pen or chalk

Pressing ham

Cutting

Use the sizing charts (next page) to determine your correct size. Then go to the key provided with Modern Classic Pencil Skirt pattern (pullout page P1) to determine the cutting line you need to use. We suggest tracing your size on pattern tracing paper. Alternatively, you can highlight the cutting lines for your size on the pattern and trim away the larger sizes. Smooth the pattern pieces and fold your fabric in half lengthwise.

All seam allowances are ⁵⁄₈″ (1.6 cm) unless otherwise noted.

These are the 4 pattern pieces that make up the Modern Classic Pencil Skirt:

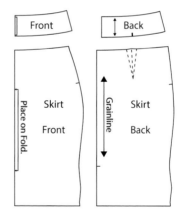

From the fashion fabric

* Cut 1 skirt front on the fabric fold.

* Cut 2 skirt backs.

* Cut 1 front waistband on the fabric fold.

* Cut 2 back waistbands.

From the lining

* Cut 1 skirt front on the fabric fold.

* Cut 2 skirt backs.

* Cut 1 front waistband on the fabric fold.

* Cut 2 back waistbands.

From the interfacing

* Cut 1 front waistband on the fold.

* Cut 2 back waistbands.

Sizing Charts

BODY MEASUREMENTS

		2	4	6	8	10	12	14	16	18	20	22
Waist	in.	26″	27″	28″	30″	31″	33″	35″	37″	39″	41″	43″
	cm	66	68.5	71.1	76.2	78.7	83.8	88.9	94	99.1	104.1	109.2
High hip	in.	32$\frac{1}{2}$″	33$\frac{1}{2}$″	34$\frac{1}{2}$″	35$\frac{1}{2}$″	37″	38$\frac{1}{2}$″	40″	42″	44″	46″	48″
	cm	82.5	85.1	87.6	90.2	94	97.8	101.6	106.7	111.8	116.8	121.9
Full hip	in.	35$\frac{1}{2}$″	36$\frac{1}{2}$″	37$\frac{1}{2}$″	38$\frac{1}{2}$″	40″	41$\frac{1}{2}$″	43″	45″	47″	49″	51″
	cm	90.2	92.7	95.2	97.8	101.6	105.4	109.2	114.3	119.4	124.5	129.5

FINISHED MEASUREMENTS

		2	4	6	8	10	12	14	16	18	20	22
Waist	in.	28$\frac{1}{2}$″	29$\frac{3}{8}$″	30$\frac{5}{8}$″	31$\frac{3}{4}$″	33$\frac{3}{8}$″	35″	36$\frac{5}{8}$″	38$\frac{7}{8}$″	41$\frac{1}{8}$″	43$\frac{1}{8}$″	45$\frac{5}{8}$″
	cm	72.4	74.7	77.7	80.5	84.8	89	93	98.6	104.6	109.7	115.8
High hip	in.	36$\frac{1}{4}$″	37$\frac{1}{4}$″	38$\frac{1}{4}$″	39$\frac{1}{4}$″	41″	42$\frac{1}{4}$″	44″	46″	48$\frac{1}{4}$″	50$\frac{1}{4}$″	52$\frac{1}{4}$″
	cm	92	94.6	97.2	99.7	103.8	107.3	112	117	122.6	127.6	132.7
Full hip	in.	37$\frac{7}{8}$″	38$\frac{7}{8}$″	39$\frac{7}{8}$″	40$\frac{7}{8}$″	42$\frac{1}{4}$″	43$\frac{7}{8}$″	45$\frac{1}{4}$″	47$\frac{1}{4}$″	49$\frac{1}{4}$″	51$\frac{1}{4}$″	53$\frac{1}{4}$″
	cm	96	98.4	101	103.5	107.3	111	115	120	125	130.2	135.3
Length	in.	20″	20″	20$\frac{1}{8}$″	20$\frac{1}{8}$″	20$\frac{1}{4}$″	20$\frac{3}{8}$″	20$\frac{1}{2}$″	20$\frac{5}{8}$″	20$\frac{3}{4}$″	20$\frac{7}{8}$″	21″
	cm	51	51	51.2	51.2	51.5	51.8	52	52.3	52.5	52.8	53.3

Preparing the Skirt

1. Interface all the waistband pieces and trace the stitching lines on the interfaced side. (This step helps ensure precision stitching.)

2. Sew the darts in the skirt back pieces. Press the darts toward the center back.

3. With right sides together, stitch the back waistband pieces to the back skirt pieces. Trim the seams to $\frac{3}{8}$″ (1 cm) and press them toward the waistband. *fig. A*

4. Attach the front waistband to the front skirt piece, with right sides together. Trim the seam to $\frac{3}{8}$″ (1 cm) and press it toward the waistband. *fig. B*

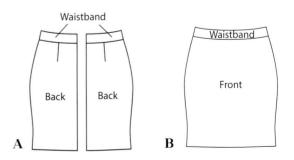

5. With right sides together, machine baste the center back seam from the top of the waistband to 1″ (2.5 cm) below the zipper stop mark.

6. Install an invisible zipper (see How to Install an Invisible Zipper, at right).

7. With right sides together, stitch the skirt front to the skirt back at the side seams. Press the seams open over a sewing ham. (Using a ham helps press the curved seams open through the hip area.)

How to Install an Invisible Zipper

1. Set your iron to a low-heat setting.

2. Open the zipper and press each side of the coil away from the zipper tape; avoid pressing directly on the coils.

3. Position the open zipper, right side down on the wrong side of the center back seam so the zipper zips to the top of the waistband. Hand baste the zipper tape to the seam allowances on both sides of the zipper opening.

4. Remove the machine basting stitches from the seam. Check to make sure the zipper operates properly.

5. Attach an invisible zipper foot to your machine and stitch each side of the zipper to the zipper stop.

6. Hand or machine stitch the bottom tapes of the zipper to the seam allowances.

7. Stitch the center back seam, below the zipper to the back slit marking.

8. Press the seam allowances open, including the unstitched seam allowances for the back slit.

Preparing the Lining

1. Sew the darts in the skirt back pieces. Press the darts towards the center back.

2. With right sides together, stitch the back waistband pieces to the back skirt pieces. Trim the seams to $3/8''$ (1 cm) and press them toward the waistband.

3. Stitch the back lining pieces, right sides together between the marked circles (the zippered area and the back slit area are not stitched). Press the seam open.

4. Attach the front waistband to the front skirt with right sides together. Trim the seam allowance to $3/8''$ (1 cm) and press it toward the waistband.

5. With right sides together, stitch the lining front to the lining back at the side seams. Press the seams open over a sewing ham.

Attaching the Skirt and Lining

1. With right sides together, pin the lining to the skirt along the top of the waistband. The lining extends $5/8''$ (1.6 cm) beyond each side of the center back opening. Baste along the marked stitching lines.

2. Stitch the seam. Press the seam allowance towards the skirt and then understitch (close to the seam, through the seam allowance) the waistband and lining seam.

3. Turn the seam allowance of the lining along the waistband and zipper seam.

4. Whipstitch the folded edge of the lining to the center opening of the waistband and along the zipper tape to the bottom of the zipper.

5. Topstitch in the waistband seam on the fashion fabric side of the skirt. (This technique is also known as *stitch-in-the-ditch*. This step defines the waistband and keeps the waistband from stretching.)

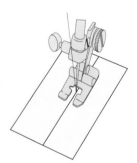

Finishing the Skirt

1. Use your favorite hemming technique to hem outside skirt.

2. Fold the back-slit seam allowances $1/4''$ (6 mm) to the wrong side and then again $3/8''$ (1 cm) to form a clean edge. Press the folded seam allowances.

3. Hem the lining using your preferred method.

4. Whipstitch the lining to the skirt along the back slit.

Enjoy your skirt!

Contributors

Looking for inspiration? These sixteen friends from the online sewing community join us in celebrating classic clothing with a contemporary spin!

Alex Florea   A former Great British Sewing Bee contestant, Alex shares her stylish and sustainable sewing journey on her blog and on Instagram.

Website: sewrendipity.com   Instagram: @sewrendipity

Photo by Alexandra Florea

Allie Jackson   Allie's modern midcentury sewing style represents the epitome of classic sewing! Follow Allie's blog, where she shares her sewing adventures.

Website: alliemjackson.com   Instagram: @helloalliej

Photo by Allie Jackson

Andrea Birkan   Andrea's love of couture sewing is evident in all her sewing projects. She is a whiz at creating unique blouses and French jackets.

Instagram: @andreabirkan

Photo by Andrea Birkan

Anita Morris   Creator of the sewing blog *Anita by Design*, Anita Morris provides sew along videos and online sewing courses along with sewing fabulous clothes for herself!

Website: anitabydesign.com   Instagram: @anitabydesign

Photo by Anita Morris

Cennetta Burwell   Creator of the popular sewing blog *The Mahogany Stylist* and a member of the Mood Fabrics' Sewing Network, Cennetta sews it all while featuring a fondness for the classics!

Blog: themahoganystylist.blogspot.com   Instagram: @cennetta_burwell

Photo by Cennetta Burwell

Dorcas Ross   This talented Texan and brand ambassador for Sew Much Fabric is slowly filling a curated closet with beautiful hand sewn and couture garments.

Blog: lonestarcouture.blogspot.com   Instagram: @lonestarcouture

Photo by Dorcas Ross

Duong Nguyen Lengerer   She's also known as Birdy and is an industrious, talented, creative and highly skilled sewist. We adore her adorable dresses! Follow Birdy's impressive sewing adventures on Instagram.

Instagram: @birdy_sew_obsessed

Photo by Duong Nguyen Lengerer

Emily Hallman   Sewist and designer Emily Hallman is recognized for creating magical coordinated garment collections.

Website: emilyhallman.com   Instagram: @emilyhallmandesigns

Photo by Emily Hallman

Jacqueline Foley   We anxiously await each and every artfully photographed creation by the marvelous sewist Jacqueline Foley!

Instagram: @ladyfoleysews

Photo by Jacqueline Foley

Karen K. Helm   With a love of midcentury patterns and accomplished couture skills, Karen Helm's perfectly sewn garments recapture the essence of the classic designers who have inspired her through the years.

Website: fiftydresses.com   Instagram: @fiftydresses

Photo by Thomas B. Helm

Karon Cooke-Euter   Karon's beautiful tops and tailored blouses recently caught our eye and we're glad they did!

Instagram: @cookeka

Photo by Karon Cooke-Euter

Lauren Taylor   This native Nashvillian has a love for all things sewing-related and a blog to prove it. An original member of The Mood Sewing Network, Lauren's huge following grows on a daily basis.

Website: lladybird.com   Instagram: @lladybird

Photo by Jenna Ledawn

Lori VanMaanan   Lori's blog, *Girls in the Garden*, details this industrious sewist's adventures. An original blogger for the Mood Sewing Network, Lori sews quilts, beautifully tailored clothes, and everything in between.

Website: girlsinthegarden.net   Instagram: @girlsinthegarden

Photo by Lori VanMaanen

Lucy VanDoorn   With a remarkable creative vision and technical prowess to match, Lucy's stunning handmade wardrobe represents the best of sewing on all levels!

Blog: myloveaffairwithsewing.com   Instagram: @myloveaffairwithsewing

Photo by Martin Mogaard

Manju Nittala   British sewing blogger, Manju is a scientist by day and a sewing diva by night! She fearlessly undertakes sewing challenges with vigor, and her expert skill set is evident in the beautiful garments she creates.

Blog: sewmanju.com   Instagram: @sewmanju

Photo by Philip Nittala / Manju Nittala

Vatsla Watkins, 1980-2019   With a background in fashion design, Vatsla's chic creations reflect a comprehensive understanding of all things sewing, pattern making and fashion design related. As a fashion designer, teacher, and freelance pattern maker, Vatsla contracted pattern making to other companies. She also taught fashion design at a local college.

Photo by Vatsla Watkins

Beth Briggs received a BA in studio art / art history from Wellesley College, and studied fashion design and illustration at RISD, Parsons (The New School), Syracuse University (Florence, Italy), and Mass College of Art. Her passion for fashion illustration has led her from Boston to New York to her new home in sunny Sarasota where she creates custom illustrations and original paintings inspired by a fashionable life.

Photo by Miss Paris Photos

Resources

Fabric Books

Baugh, Gail. *The Fashion Designer's Textile Directory*, 2nd edition. Hauppauge, New York: B.E.S. Publishing, 2018.

Hallett, Clive and Amanda Johnston. *Fabric for Fashion: The Complete Guide.* London: Laurence King Publishing, 2014.

Mood Designer Fabrics. *The Mood Guide to Fabric and Fashion.* New York: Harry N. Abrams, 2015.

Walnes, Tilly. *Tilly and the Buttons: Stretch!: Make Yourself Comfortable Sewing with Knit Fabrics.* London: Quadrille Publishing, 2018.

Willard, Dana. *Fabrics A–Z: The Essential Guide to Choosing and Using Fabric for Sewing.* New York: Stewart, Tabori and Chang, 2012.

Fabric Vendors

If you are lucky enough to live near independently operated brick and mortar fabric stores, we encourage you to patronize these businesses. The sensory experience and personal customer service is invaluable. For online fabric shopping, we recommend the following businesses. Remember to request a fabric swatch until you get the hang of online shopping.

B&J Fabrics   bandjfabrics.com

Blackbird Fabrics   blackbirdfabrics.com

Britex Fabrics   britexfabrics.com

Elliot Berman   elliottbermantextiles.com

Emma One Sock   emmaonesock.com

Fabric.com   fabric.com

Fabric Mart   fabricmartfabrics.com

Farmhouse Fabrics   farmhousefabrics.com

Fashion Fabrics Club   fashionfabricsclub.com

Gorgeous Fabrics   gorgeousfabrics.com

Marcy Tilton   marcytilton.com

Mendel Goldberg Fabrics   mendelgoldbergfabrics.com

Mood Fabrics   moodfabrics.com

Michael Levine   lowpricefabric.com

Promenade Fine Fabrics   promenadefinefabrics.com

Sew Much Fabrics   stores.smfabric.com

Stonemountain & Daughter Fabrics   stonemountainfabric.com

Style Maker Fabrics   stylemakerfabrics.com

Vogue Fabrics   voguefabricsstore.com

Fabric Shopping Around the Globe

Casa dei Tessuti   Florence, Milan, and Rome, Italy

General Diff   Paris, France

Janssens & Janssens   Paris, France

Liberty of London   London, UK

Linton Tweeds   Carlisle, UK

Tessuti   Sydney and Melbourne, Australia

Valli Tessuti Alta Moda   Milan, Bologna, Florence, and Rome, Italy

Trims, Tools, and Notions

Bias Bespoke Supply Co.   biasbespoke.com
Owned, curated and run by professional tailors in New York, featuring sewing supplies for fashion lovers.

Etsy   etsy.com
Features a constantly changing list of online vendors. We recommend visiting Etsy's website and bookmarking a few favorites. We have purchased lovely jacquard, appliqués, and twill tape from Etsy.

Fashion Sewing Supply   fashionsewingsupply.com
The place to find the best professional-grade interfacings.

M&J Trimming   mjtrim.com
Has a spectacular selection of trims at its physical and online stores.

Mokuba
Sells beautiful ribbons and trims at its store on 137 West 38th Street, New York, NY 10018. No website sales are available.

The Sewing Place   thesewingplace.com
Offers Petersham ribbon in dozens of colors and sizes.

Susan Khalje Couture   susankhalje.com
Offers a wide variety of patterns and supplies for all your dressmaking needs.

Related Articles, Videos, and Online Classes

Bluprint tutorials   Online classes: You can learn to do anything on mybluprint.com. Below are a few invaluable online classes we recommend:

JULIA GARZA   "WANT PERFECT FIT? THEN YOU GOTTA MAKE A MUSLIN"

PAM W. HOWARD   "THE CLASSIC TAILORED SHIRT"

SUSAN KHALJE   "THE COUTURE DRESS"

LORNA KNIGHT   "THE ICONIC TWEED JACKET"

MARCY AND KATHERINE TILTON   "THE ULTIMATE T-SHIRT: FITTING AND CONSTRUCTION"

ANGELA WOLF   "SEWING DESIGNER JEANS"

Maria Denmark   Article: "An Easy Full Bust Adjustment (FBA) for No-Dart Fronts."

MARIADENMARK.COM > *search* "EASY FBA" > *click on article title*

Sew News   Article series: "Robson Coat Sew-Along"

SEWNEWS.COM > BLOG > *search* "ROBSON COAT" > *click on article title, starting with* "Week 1"

Susan Khalje Couture   Online class: "The Classic French Jacket"

SUSANKHALJE.COM > VIDEOS > "THE CLASSIC FRENCH JACKET"

Threads magazine   Videos (Petersham ribbon waistband)

SUSAN KHALJE   *Learning Couture Techniques for Building a Waistband.* | THREADSMAGAZINE.COM > *search* "COUTURE BUILDING WAISTBAND" > *click on video title*

EVAMARIE GOMEZ AND STEPHANI MILLER   *How to Shape Petersham to a Curve.* | THREADSMAGAZINE.COM > *search* "SHAPE PETERSHAM" > *click on video title*

Sewing Instruction and Alteration Books

Coffin, David P. *Shirtmaking: Developing Skills for Fine Sewing.* Newtown, Connecticut: Taunton Press, 1998.

Emodi, Barbara. *SEW … The Garment-Making Book of Knowledge.* Lafayette, California: Stash Books, 2018.

Gunn, Sarah and Julie Starr. *The Tunic Bible.* Lafayette, California: C&T Publishing, 2016.

King, Kenneth D. *Kenneth D. King's Smart Fitting Solutions: Foolproof Techniques to Fit Any Figure.* Newtown, Connecticut: Taunton Press, 2018.

Liechty, Elizabeth, Judith Rasband, and Della Pottberg-Steineckert. *Fitting and Pattern Alteration: A Multi-Method Approach to the Art of Style Selection, Fitting, and Alteration*, 3rd edition. New York: Fairchild Books, 2016.

Miller, Ellen W. *Creating Couture Embellishment.* London: Laurence King Publishing, 2017.

Prakash, Deepika. *PatternReview.com 1,000 Clever Sewing Shortcuts and Tips.* Minneapolis, Minnesota: Creative Publishing International, 2010.

Palmer, Pati, Marta Alto, and Barbara Weiland. *Fit for Real People: Sew Great Clothes Using Any Pattern.* Vancouver, Washington: Palmer/Pletsch Publishing, 1998.

St. Germaine, Tasia. *The Sewtionary: An A to Z Guide to 101 Sewing Techniques and Definitions.* Cincinnati, Ohio: KP Craft, 2014.

Shaeffer, Claire. *Couture Sewing Techniques.* Newtown, Connecticut: Taunton Press, 2011.

Veblen, Sarah. *The Complete Photo Guide to Perfect Fitting.* Minneapolis, Minnesota: Creative Publishing International, 2012.

von Nordheim, Thomas. *Vintage Couture Tailoring.* Marlborough, UK: Crowood Press, 2012.

Zieman, Nancy. *Pattern Fitting with Confidence.* Cincinnati, Ohio: KP Craft, 2008.

About the Authors

SARAH GUNN

Since 2011, blogger and author Sarah Gunn has inspired thousands of women across the globe, nurturing their creative spirit through her fashion sewing blog, *Goodbye Valentino*. After a year of blogging about creating a hand-curated wardrobe, Sarah was approached by New York's Mood Fabrics, the *Project Runway* go-to fabric store, and became an original member of its online sewing network.

Coauthor of the award-winning book *The Tunic Bible*, Sarah has served as an ambassador for SVP International (Singer Viking Pfaff) for the Pfaff Brand, a contributor to the Coats & Clark website and PBS series *It's Sew Easy*.

Recognized for creating the "Ready-to-Wear Fast," Sarah has led dedicated followers through the RTW Fast 365-day pledge to sew rather than shop with panache.

Inspired by favorite designers, beautiful textiles as well as her own designs, Sarah's sought-after style encourages women to think beyond ready-to-wear shopping.

JULIE STARR

Julie resides near Charleston, South Carolina. She is coauthor of *The Tunic Bible* and is a perennially favorite contributor to the 400,000+ global member website Sewing Pattern Review where her clothing has won six consecutive annual awards based on member votes and has been profiled as their "Member in Focus."

Julie successfully completed three years participation in the *Goodbye Valentino* Ready-to-Wear Fast. Her professional career in custom luxury homebuilding on Kiawah Island, South Carolina, provides a skill set which translates easily to garment design and construction. The natural beauty of South Carolina's low-country beaches, tidal marsh, and diverse flora and fauna, along with the history and charm of historic Charleston, are reflected in her work and provide much of her design inspiration.

Also by Sarah Gunn and Julie Starr:

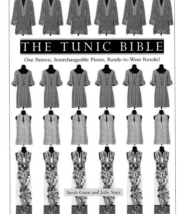

Visit Sarah online and follow on social media!

BLOG: GOODBYEVALENTINO.COM · INSTAGRAM: @GOODBYEVALENTINO
PINTEREST: /GOODBYEVALENTINO · FACEBOOK: /GOODBYEVALENTINO

Follow Julie on social media!

INSTAGRAM: @JULIE__STARR · PINTEREST: /JULIESTARRSEWS
